Barrels of bourbon age in a rickhouse
at Heaven Hill in Bardstown, Kentucky.
(Photo courtesy of Heaven Hill)

BARREL STRENGTH (ADJ.):

Premium whiskey straight from the cask, uncut and unadulterated; experienced at its fullest potential and prized by connoisseurs; the real deal.

BARREL STRENGTH BOURBON

THE EXPLOSIVE GROWTH OF AMERICA'S WHISKEY

CARLA HARRIS CARLTON

CLERISY PRESS

Barrel Strength Bourbon:
The Explosive Growth of America's Whiskey

For further information, contact the publisher:

CLERISY PRESS
An imprint of AdventureKEEN
2204 First Avenue S., Suite 102
Birmingham, AL 35233
clerisypress.com

Library of Congress Cataloging-in-Publication Data

Names: Carlton, Carla Harris, 1966– author.
Title: Barrel strength bourbon : the explosive growth of America's whiskey /
Carla Harris Carlton.
Description: Birmingham, AL : Clerisy Press, [2017]
Identifiers: LCCN 2016041259 | ISBN 978-1-57860-575-0
ISBN 978-1-57860-576-7 (eISBN)
Subjects: LCSH: Bourbon whiskey—Kentucky—History.
Classification: LCC TP605 .C28 2017 | DDC 663/.52—dc23
LC record available at lccn.loc.gov/2016041259

Distributed by Publishers Group West
Printed in China
First edition, second printing 2018

Editor: Lady Vowell Smith
Project editor: Ritchey Halphen
Cover design: Travis Bryant
Text design: Steve Sullivan
Cartography: Scott McGrew
Proofreader: Susan Roberts McWilliams
Indexer: Ann Weik Cassar/Cassar Technical Services

Cover photos: front, © The Len/Shutterstock; back, Brown-Forman
Interior photos: as noted on page and as follows: pages 10–11, Brown-Forman;
pages 26–27, Beam Suntory; pages 30–31 and pages 54–55, Kentucky Distillers'
Association; pages 82–83, Heaven Hill; pages 106–107, Kentucky Department of
Travel; pages 150–151, Carla Carlton; pages 162–163, Heaven Hill

DEDICATION

For my mother, who has listened to far more of my stories
than I will ever write, and my father, who never drank anything
stronger than black coffee but was proud of me anyway.

Write drunk; edit sober.*

*This quote has been widely attributed to Ernest Hemingway, but most fact-checkers
now agree that the actual source was writer and editor Peter De Vries (1910–1993).
In any case, it's sound advice.

TABLE OF CONTENTS

ACKNOWLEDGMENTS

THIS BOOK IS the culmination of years of study—and I'm not just referring to research done while sitting at a bar.

I owe a debt of gratitude to the many folks in the Kentucky bourbon industry who let me tag along while they did their work and answered dozens of questions, among them Master Distillers Jim Rutledge, Jimmy and Eddie Russell, Chris Morris, Harlen Wheatley, Fred Noe, Charlie Downs, Parker and Craig Beam, Denny Potter, Wes Henderson, Steve Beam, John Pogue, and Paul Tomaszewski; Maker's Mark's Bill Samuels Jr. and Rob Samuels; Heaven Hill's Larry Kass and Josh Hafer; Sazerac's Amy Preske; and Four Roses' Karen Kushner.

The Kentucky Distillers' Association (KDA), particularly president Eric Gregory and Adam Johnson, manager of the Kentucky Bourbon Trail program, provided invaluable data and insight. The Kentucky Bourbon Timeline commissioned by the KDA (tinyurl.com/kybourbontimeline) was also a great resource, as was *Kentucky Bourbon Whiskey: An American Heritage*, by my friend Michael Veach.

Some quotes in this book were taken from *Kentucky Bourbon Tales*, an oral history project produced by the Louie B. Nunn Center for Oral History at the University of Kentucky Libraries and the KDA, for which I interviewed Four Roses' Jim Rutledge and Al Young. For more information, visit nunncenter.org/bourbon.

The KDA also provided photographs for this book, as did a number of individual distilleries (as noted on page) and the Kentucky Department of Travel. (See the copyright page for additional credits.)

Thank you to Jerry Rogers, whose invitation to join the Bourbon Board of Directors at Party Mart has given me many wonderful bourbon-education opportunities.

Thanks also to Stacey Yates for making the introduction that led to this book, and to Tim W. Jackson, senior acquisitions editor at AdventureKEEN, for his patience, his kindness, and his skill in fending off the production team.

Thank you to all of the teachers who honed my use of language, including, but not limited to, Nancy Basham, Pauline Weis, Brenda "The Grammar Goddess" Martin, and James D. Ausenbaugh.

Thank you to my mother, Joyce J. Harris, who read to me every day when I was little, and to my father, Carl Harris, who demonstrated that anything worth doing is worth doing right. Their love and belief in me taught me to believe in myself. I wish my father had lived to see this book, but his delight that I was writing it is enough.

Finally, thank you to my two bright and beautiful children, Harper and Clay, who inspire me to be a better person (and who shot some of the photos in this book), and to my wonderfully supportive husband, Chad, who *is* a better person but puts up with me anyway. I love you all more than I can say. Cheers!

XIV

Interior of Brown-Forman's office on Louisville's Whiskey Row,
circa 1890 (Photo courtesy of Brown-Forman)

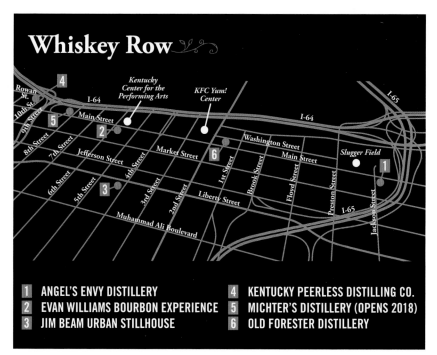

Whiskey Row

1 ANGEL'S ENVY DISTILLERY
2 EVAN WILLIAMS BOURBON EXPERIENCE
3 JIM BEAM URBAN STILLHOUSE
4 KENTUCKY PEERLESS DISTILLING CO.
5 MICHTER'S DISTILLERY (OPENS 2018)
6 OLD FORESTER DISTILLERY

3

These projects represent just a fraction of the more than $400 million that distilling companies have invested in capital projects in Kentucky since 2008: new stills, bottling lines, and warehouses, and larger visitor centers. And another $630 million in projects is planned over the next five years.

A new wave of craft distilleries is rising not just in Kentucky but across the country. Kentucky actually ranks only 11th on the list of states' total numbers of distillers nationwide. But its numbers include all of the industry giants—Brown-Forman, Jim Beam, Wild Turkey, Four Roses, Buffalo Trace, Maker's Mark, and Heaven Hill among them—and, as a result, Kentucky produces about 95% of the world's supply of bourbon.

Since the year 2000, that production has increased by more than 315%, to 1.89 million barrels in 2015. And more than 6.6 million barrels are currently maturing in warehouses in the Bluegrass State.

People aren't just drinking Kentucky bourbon; they're coming to visit it. In 2016, the Kentucky Bourbon Trail and Kentucky Bourbon Trail Craft Tour recorded 1,065,961 visits, breaking the 1 million mark for the first time. That number is expected to grow as more distilleries join the tours.

(Continued on page 7)

KENTUCKY CRAFT DISTILLERIES
(Photos courtesy of the Kentucky Distillers'
Association except as noted)

Top row, left to right across the spread:
MB Roland Kentucky bourbon, The Old Pogue
Distillery, still at Old Pogue, barrels at Copper
& Kings American Brandy Co. *Middle row, left to
right across the spread:* Boone County Distilling's
Tanner's Curse (photo courtesy of Boone County
Distilling Co.), Corsair product samples, close-
up of Wilderness Trail still. *Bottom row, left to
right across the spread:* New Riff Distillery,
Willett Distillery, on the job at Limestone Trace

6

EVAN WILLIAMS BOURBON EXPERIENCE

A five-story bottle keeps the "bourbon" flowing at the Evan Williams Bourbon Experience in downtown Louisville, where guests may sample premium products made by Heaven Hill *(right)*. (Photos courtesy of Heaven Hill)

(Continued from page 3)

"I think some of that has to do with the millennial generation wanting authenticity and being entrepreneurs, but also the older business generation realizing how important it is to promote your differentiating points," says Stacey Yates, vice president of marketing communications for the Louisville Convention & Visitors Bureau. "Not to dis the chains, but most travelers want that authentic experience now."

Yates has helped to burnish the reputation of what was long regarded as a rough-edged spirit by creating Louisville's Urban Bourbon Trail, in which member restaurants not only feature at least 50 kinds of bourbon but also use it as an ingredient in fine cuisine and serious cocktails. Social media and mass media have also done their part to make bourbon cool again, she says. "You can't underestimate the power of Don Draper drinking an old-fashioned on *Mad Men*. You just can't. It did for Kentucky what *Sideways* did for wine country."

The longstanding annual Kentucky Bourbon Festival in Bardstown, the Bourbon Capital of the World, has been joined by other high-profile bourbon events, including the Bourbon Classic in Louisville, in which top mixologists and some of Kentucky's finest chefs create classic pairings; and the Kentucky Distillers' Association's Bourbon Affair, a weeklong "fantasy camp" that offers enthusiasts exclusive opportunities such as the chance to fish with Jim Beam Master Distiller Fred Noe or shoot skeet at Wild Turkey with Master Distiller Jimmy Russell. Each year, the KDA offers 50 Golden Tickets that offer a combination of events and experiences. In 2014, the Affair's inaugural year, the 50 tickets sold out in a week at $1,350 each. In 2016, at $1,595 apiece, they sold out in 15 minutes.

Additional proof of bourbon's appeal could be found in the Fantasy Gifts section of the 2015 Neiman Marcus Christmas Book, where "eye-popping, jaw-dropping dreams come true." Nestled between a two-day California coast road trip on custom motorcycles with actor Keanu Reeves ($150,000) and an exploration of the edge of space in a capsule lifted by a high-altitude balloon to 100,000 feet ($90,000) was the Orphan Barrel Project gift, a trip for six to Stitzel-Weller in Louisville to sample rare bourbon finds and create two new blends to be bottled with custom labels. In all, the recipient was promised 24 bottles each of the two blends and the six other Orphan Barrel varieties; a bespoke whiskey cabinet crafted in Kentucky; barware; a leather-bound book about the whiskey; and three nights of luxury accommodations, meals, and first-class travel. The price? A cool $125,000.

The popularity of bourbon is further evident in the variety of businesses jumping on the bourbon bandwagon. There are bourbon chocolates, bourbon-scented soaps and lip balm, furniture made from bourbon barrels, and a new bottled water called Old Limestone that is being marketed as "the official companion of Kentucky Bourbon." Kentucky grain farmers are even starting to talk about "terroir."

We've come a long way from the time when former Four Roses Master Distiller Jim Rutledge (who was then working at Seagram) and an associate asked for bourbon at a restaurant outside Kentucky. "We both took a drink and almost spit it out," he says. "We thought, 'God, what's wrong with this? Is it poisonous?' And then we realized that it wasn't poison—it was just Scotch."

Jim Rutledge, former Master Distiller at Four Roses (Photo: Carla Carlton)

Scotch whisky (without the *e*) has dominated the world whiskey market for centuries. That began to change, Rutledge says, when the American bourbon industry started focusing on premium single-barrel and small-batch products. The pendulum has swung so far in the other direction, in fact, that now Scotch producers are highlighting their lighter, mellower whiskies. One Scotch distiller he encountered at trade events has begun aging his spirit in new oak barrels rather than in the used ones typical to Scotch.

"I'd ask some of these other distillers or blenders what they thought about it, and they'd say"—here, Rutledge puts on an expression of disgust—" 'It tastes like bourbon.' They were really irritated. They didn't like it at all. You'd see them turning red. They'd get mad. But that's the biggest compliment of all, when Scotch starts to emulate what we're doing."

Can this bourbon boom continue? I'll try to answer that question in the following pages. Along the way, I'll take you on a short journey through the history of the amber spirit and introduce you to some of the industry's biggest personalities. I'll explain how bourbon is made and how it differs from other kinds of whiskey. I'll teach you how to taste bourbon, and I'll give you a vocabulary to describe what you're tasting. If that sounds a lot like school, take heart: there won't be a test, and the homework is delicious.

9

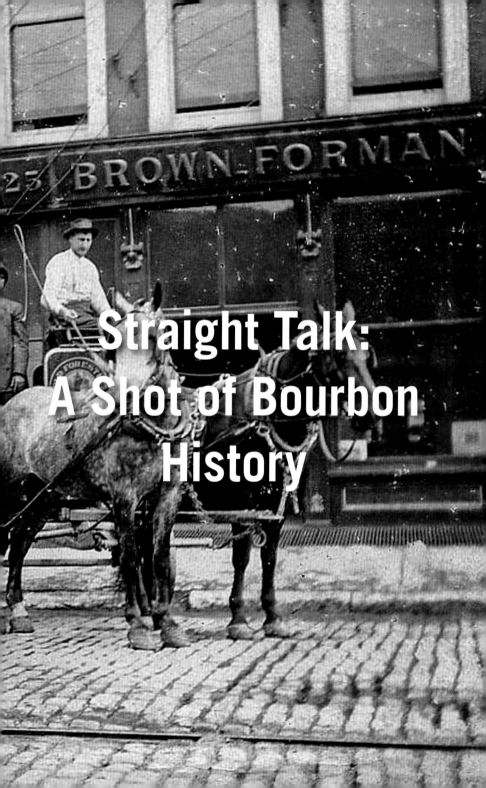

Straight Talk:
A Shot of Bourbon History

"I have never in my life seen a Kentuckian who didn't have a gun, a pack of cards, and a jug of whiskey."

—*US President Andrew Jackson*

TRUE OR FALSE: Bourbon can be made only in Kentucky.

If you answered "true," you're not alone. You're also wrong. But don't feel bad; I've encountered plenty of people who firmly hold that conviction—including bartenders in Kentucky who should know better. The truth is, you can make bourbon in any state, as long as it's one of the United States of America. The confusion is easy to understand, however, as Kentucky produces all but about 5% of the bourbon in the world.

Now let's further test your knowledge of bourbon with a short multiple-choice quiz. Yes, you in the back with your hand up: how can I help you? The introduction said there wouldn't be any tests? Well, no one really reads the introduction, do they? If you did, I'm sorry. I lied. *Ahem.*

1. Who made the very first bourbon?	2. When was the very first bourbon made?	3. Where did bourbon get its name?
a. Jacob Beam	a. 1783	a. Bourbon County, Kentucky
b. Elijah Craig	b. 1792	b. Bourbon County, Virginia
c. Evan Williams	c. 1821	c. Bourbon Street in New Orleans
d. I don't know.	d. I don't know.	d. I don't know.

The correct answer to all three: **d.** Don't be offended, by the way— I don't mean that *you* don't know the answers to these questions; I mean that *I* don't.

The truth is, despite what you may have read or heard elsewhere, nobody knows for sure who "invented" bourbon, or when or how it got its name. People were too busy just trying to survive back then to write much down. What we do know is that people have been making bourbon in Kentucky since before there even was a Kentucky, when the land that is now the Bluegrass State was part of Virginia.

What follows are some other things we know—or our best guesses. Much of this information was gleaned from bourbon historian Michael Veach's excellent book, *Kentucky Bourbon Whiskey: An American Heritage; The Kentucky Encyclopedia*, edited by John Kleber; the Kentucky Bourbon Timeline, commissioned by the Kentucky Distillers' Association; and interviews with Brown-Forman Master Distiller Chris Morris, who conducts a Bourbon Academy several times per year at the Woodford Reserve Distillery.

The Birth of Bourbon

The earliest settlers brought stills with them to the land that would eventually become Kentucky when they migrated west in the 1770s. Fort Harrod, the first permanent settlement in this new territory, soon became known as Harrodsburg, and when the Virginia legislature established Kentucky County in 1776, Harrodsburg became the county seat.

Colonists had been distilling spirits since their arrival in New England. One notable early distiller was George Washington. Like most of the colonists, he initially distilled rum. At Mount Vernon, his plantation manager, a Scot, is said to have persuaded him to plant rye and start making whiskey. An influx of Scots-Irish and German immigrants, in fact, helped to lay the foundations for the whiskey industry. One of them was Jacob Beam, who was attracted to the Nelson County area by its plentiful limestone-rich streams. Nelson County's seat, Bardstown, which was established in 1780 and is Kentucky's second oldest city, would eventually become known as the Bourbon Capital of the World.

In those early years, though, just about every farmer would have been distilling his excess grain harvest into whiskey, which became a form of currency. Transporting grain to market was difficult, but one packhorse could carry the equivalent of a quarter-ton of grain once it had been transformed into two 20-gallon kegs of juice.

13

Corn was especially plentiful in this new world. It grew so successfully on Dunmore's Island, a small island in the Ohio River settled by George Rogers Clark in 1778, that residents renamed it Corn Island. Five years later, in 1783, those settlers moved ashore and founded the city of Louisville, named for King Louis XVI of France, whose government had aided the colonists against England in the Revolutionary War. Farther east, another area of what was still Virginia had been given a French name in gratitude to and honor of Louis XVI's royal house: Bourbon County. In 1792, it became part of the new state—or, if you want to be technical, the new commonwealth—of Kentucky.

Around about this time, a man whose name you'll recognize from a bourbon bottle, Evan Williams, built a distillery on the banks of the Ohio in Louisville. Williams is often referred to as Kentucky's first distiller, but this claim cannot be proved. "The fact is," Veach writes, "that we may never know the identity of Kentucky's first distiller." Because distilled spirits weren't taxed, there are no government records from these early days.

That changed in 1790, when Congress voted to take on any states' debts remaining from the Revolutionary War—and to pay them by levying a tax on alcohol. (This began a practice that persists today: with the exception of the Spanish-American War, debts from every American war have been paid with alcohol-tax revenue.)

We may not be able to pinpoint the year when Evan Williams started distilling, but we do know that in 1797 he was elected to Louisville's Board of Trustees, and, more important, he was appointed harbormaster, one of the most influential positions in the city. The same limestone rock shelves that made Kentucky's streams so good for bourbon making had also made Louisville a mandatory stop for southbound river traffic: the Ohio River had carved out a series of rapids here that, over 2 miles, dropped the water level 26 feet.

Boats were unloaded at a harbor above the Falls of the Ohio, and they and their freight were portaged below the falls to continue their journey. The harbor was small and heavily used; as a result, boats had to be unloaded and moved within 48 hours. The harbormaster was in charge of making sure this happened. Louisville was already a major shipping center, and it was about to become even more important.

In 1803, President Thomas Jefferson decided to buy Louisiana, a purchase that opened up trade routes all the way to New Orleans. (That same year, Meriwether Lewis and Louisvillian William Clark departed from Louisville on a four-year tour of this new territory that would take them all the way to the Pacific. Among their supplies: 120 gallons of whiskey.)

At this point, whiskey, and anything else someone wanted to sell or trade, was transported by flatboat. These simple vessels—which, as their name implies, were essentially flat-bottomed rectangles—could easily be built by farmers to take their harvest downriver. With nothing to power them but the current, however, flatboats were a one-way ticket.

{ *Just* A SIP }

Once a farmer arrived in New Orleans, he would sell his boat as well as its contents. The buyers didn't need boats, however; they needed the lumber. (Many of the oldest shotgun-style houses in New Orleans are said to have been built with Kentucky wood that arrived in the form of a flatboat.)

15

To get back home, sellers faced a long and often dangerous trek; if someone was hiking north from New Orleans, chances were good that he was carrying a sack of money. To increase their odds of arriving alive, many Kentuckians bought horses—the fastest ones they could find—to make the trip. Some say this was the beginning of the Thoroughbred industry in Kentucky.

Fortunately, a man named Robert Fulton was busy working on a boat that would be able to make the round-trip. He developed the first commercial steamboat in 1807, and in 1815, a steamboat made the first excursion upriver from New Orleans to Louisville. (The city of Louisville owns the only authentic steamer from the great American steamboat era that is still in operation—the *Belle of Louisville*. She turned 100 in 2014 and still plies the Ohio River at the dazzling top speed of 11 miles per hour.) Steam would also be harnessed to distill alcohol as distilleries adopted new technologies during the 19th century.

The French had long been aging brandy and cognac in oak barrels charred on the inside to give them flavor and color. At some point in these early 1800s, Kentucky distillers began using this same method to make whiskey, which added caramel, vanilla, and oak flavors to the spirit and gave it a distinctive amber color.

One popular legend holds that the man who came up with the idea of charring the insides of barrels to enhance the flavor of bourbon was the Reverend Elijah Craig. Now, the Reverend Craig was a real person, a man of the cloth who fled from Virginia to Kentucky because of religious persecution and built a distillery in 1789. But there is no proof that he intentionally charred barrels to improve his whiskey's flavor, and even the legends surrounding him don't make a lot of sense. One story says that after a barn fire charred some staves, Craig was too cheap to throw them out and serendipitously discovered that barrels constructed from these staves made his whiskey better. But why, Chris Morris asks, would staves burn only on one side? Another story says the frugal Craig often reused barrels and charred the insides to eliminate the flavors of whatever they had originally held, whether that was fish or pickles. But barrels were made specifically for certain uses, Morris says, and no one would ever use a fish barrel to hold whiskey.

According to Veach, the earliest known mention of charring a barrel is found in an 1826 letter to a distiller from a Lexington grocer ordering more barrels of whiskey and adding, "if the barrels should be burnt upon the inside, say only a 16th of an inch, that it will much improve it." Veach thinks it's more likely that a grocer or wholesale whiskey merchant, not a distiller, came up with the idea of aging American whiskey in charred barrels after noticing that the large French population of New Orleans favored imported brandy and cognac, both barreled-aged spirits, over local unaged corn whiskey.

One whiskey pioneer who did write things down was Dr. James Crow, who immigrated to Kentucky from Scotland in the 1820s to work at the Old Oscar Pepper Distillery in Woodford County (now Woodford Reserve Distillery). He wanted to learn as much as possible about all of the variables that affect whiskey production so that he could improve the product, and he took copious notes so that his methods could be replicated. Although

HOW DID BOURBON GET ITS NAME?

Again, nobody knows for sure, but the oldest legend is that the spirit was named for Bourbon County, Kentucky. Supposedly merchants in New Orleans found that whiskey invoiced in Limestone, in Bourbon County, Kentucky, was the tastiest, and "Bourbon County" whiskey eventually became known simply as "bourbon whiskey" or "bourbon." Bourbon historian Michael Veach, however, notes that Limestone was part of Bourbon County for only a short time while Kentucky was still part of Virginia, and because the round-trip to New Orleans took a year or more, there would not have been enough shipments invoiced to Limestone to allow that connection to be made. Limestone (now Maysville) had been part of Mason County, Kentucky, for more than 30 years when the Maysville firm of Stout and Adams advertised "Bourbon Whiskey by the barrel or keg" in a newspaper in 1821—the earliest documented use of the term.

Another theory says that people drinking the aged spirit in New Orleans started asking for "Bourbon Street whiskey," which got shortened to "bourbon." In any case, *bourbon* came to mean excellent whiskey from Kentucky.

17

the Oscar Pepper Distillery's output was small, Dr. Crow's whiskey, Old Crow, became nationally known for its high quality.

"Wall Street for Whiskey"

To accommodate the growing number of steamboats, the city of Louisville built a canal that allowed the boats to bypass the Falls of the Ohio. River traffic grew exponentially with the opening of the Portland Canal in 1830, as did Louisville's population. By 1850, Louisville was one of the 12 largest cities in America, bigger even than Chicago. The arrival of railroads made Louisville even more important as a transportation hub, with lines connecting the city to points north and west.

If you operated a distillery anywhere in the region, you shipped it from Louisville. Whiskey interests from all over opened offices and warehouses along a 12-block stretch of Main Street near the Ohio River that became known as Whiskey Row.

18

George Garvin Brown, cofounder of Brown-Forman
distillery (Photo courtesy of Brown-Forman)

Whiskey Row was also the home of rectifiers, who created new products either by blending several whiskeys together or by blending whiskey with neutral grain spirits. While some of these products were legitimate, it was easy to tamper with them since bourbon was sold directly from a barrel. There was no way of knowing exactly what you were going to get, even from reputable distillers, because one batch could differ from the previous one.

In 1870, a young Louisville distiller named George Garvin Brown landed on a solution to the problems of consistency and potential tampering. His Old Forrester Bourbon, named for a Union Army hero, Dr. William Forrester, was the first bourbon to be sold exclusively in bottles. (Incidentally, Dr. Forrester was not old; he was probably in his early 30s. "Old" denoted that the bourbon was aged, which implied quality.) At some point in history, Old Forester lost one of its *R*s, but it is still the flagship brand of the Brown-Forman distillery. Bottled bourbon did not become common until after 1904, when Michael J. Owens patented a machine that could make four uniform bottles per second.

Several other measures enacted in the late 1800s and early 1900s were designed to protect consumers and ensure authenticity in bourbon production. The Bottled-in-Bond Act of 1897 developed "Standards of Identity for Distilled Spirits," among them that spirits had to be produced by one distiller in one distilling season at one US distillery, which was to be identified on the label; had to be aged in a federally bonded warehouse for at least four years; and had to be bottled at 100 proof. The "federally bonded" part made the government responsible for guaranteeing that the standards were met. Bonded warehouses were padlocked, and only US Treasury agents had a key.

In 1906, the Pure Food and Drug Act required that all products, including whiskey, carry a label that listed their contents. But what was "pure whiskey"? The chief chemist for the U.S. Department of Agriculture decided it was a spirit distilled from grain that was aged in oak barrels and had nothing added but pure water; anything else would have to be labeled as "imitation whiskey." This upset the rectifiers, who were putting neutral grain spirits, flavoring, coloring, and who-knows-what-all into their whiskeys. President William Howard Taft finally settled the question "What is whiskey?" with the Taft Decision of 1909.

{ *Just* A SIP }

According to the Taft Decision, "straight whiskey" was to be made only from grain (not fruit or molasses) and water, and whiskey flavored with other spirits would be defined as "blended." Taft allowed the terms bourbon *and* rye *for identifying the dominant grain; the language was later expanded to account for grains such as wheat. And now you know something that President Taft did besides commission an oversize bathtub in the White House to accommodate his 340-pound girth.*

By the turn of the 20th century, there were nearly 100 whiskey-related concerns operating on and near Whiskey Row in Louisville, according to the Louisville City Directory, and not just from Kentucky; they also hailed from places like Cincinnati, Chicago, and New York. "This was the greatest accumulation of whiskey companies in the world in one place at one time," Chris Morris says. "It was like Wall Street for whiskey."

Unfortunately for both Wall Streets, big crashes were coming.

From Famine to Feast to Famine

The growth of distilling—and of cities, for that matter—in the early 1900s was not welcomed by everyone. A new temperance movement that blamed alcohol consumption for society's ills was gaining momentum. Women played a large role in this movement. Somewhat ironically, one of the most well-known members of the Woman's Christian Temperance Union was a native Kentuckian. Carry A. Nation, whose first husband was an alcoholic, smashed up saloons with her famous hatchet from December 1900 until her death in 1911. Joining religious protestors were some wealthy business owners who believed that sober workers were harder workers.

Prohibition supporters got a boost when the United States entered World War I in 1917 and President Woodrow Wilson instituted a temporary wartime prohibition during which distillers could produce only industrial alcohol. That same year, Congress submitted for state ratification the 18th Amendment, which banned the manufacture, transportation, and sale—but not use—of intoxicating liquors. The amendment received the support of the required three-quarters of US states in 11 months.

The 18th Amendment was ratified on January 16, 1919, and took effect a year later. In October 1919, Congress passed the National Prohibition Act—commonly known as the Volstead Act, in reference to Rep. Andrew Volstead of Minnesota, the chairman of the House Judiciary Committee—which provided guidelines for enforcing Prohibition.

Alcohol could be legally sold only for medicinal purposes, and just six distilleries in the entire country had licenses to produce this "medicine." Doctors could prescribe 1 pint of 100-proof whiskey per patient every 10 days. Needless to say, a lot of people fell ill in those days.

Generally speaking, the provisions of Prohibition were enforced much more strongly in rural areas, where residents tended to support them, than in urban ones. (This dichotomy continues even today in Bible Belt states like Kentucky, where, despite its prodigious bourbon production, 77 of its 120 counties were classified as dry in March 2016, according to the state Department of Alcoholic Beverage Control.) Overall, rather than curtailing distilling, Prohibition just shifted control of it to the criminal element. The 1920s saw the rise of bootleggers, speakeasies, and gangsters such as Al Capone, who reportedly earned $60 million annually from illegal operations associated with alcohol.

21

{ *Just* A SIP }

Al Capone was a frequent guest at The Seelbach Hotel in Louisville, as was Cincinnati mobster George Remus, known popularly as the "King of the Bootleggers." Remus, who befriended writer F. Scott Fitzgerald, who was stationed with the Army at nearby Camp Taylor, was said to have inspired Jay Gatsby in Fitzgerald's 1925 masterpiece, The Great Gatsby. *Fitzgerald's characters Tom and Daisy Buchanan were married in Louisville at "The Muhlbach."*

Prohibition cost the country lots of jobs, not just in the distilling industry but also in ancillary businesses such as cooperages, bottle manufacturers, and taverns—even farmers were affected. By the 1932 presidential election, with the country in the midst of the Great Depression, it was clear that the so-called "Noble Experiment" had failed, and candidates for both major parties promised to do away with it.

Under President Franklin Roosevelt, Congress proposed the 21st Amendment, which repealed the 18th, in February 1933, and the states ratified it in December 1933. It's worth noting, historian Veach says, that the 18th Amendment is thus far the only amendment that limited the freedoms of American citizens—and the only amendment that has ever been repealed. It's also worth noting that the 21st Amendment ceded control over alcoholic beverages to the states, which led to a confusing and inconsistent array of laws that still exists today.

Many distilleries never reopened after Repeal. The 1930s saw lots of consolidation as large distilling companies bought up smaller ones; it also saw the creation of one startup that would prove to be very successful: Heaven Hill, which was founded in 1935 by the Shapira brothers and which today is the nation's largest independent family-owned and -operated distilled spirits producer.

The distilling industry as a whole had really no more than started gearing back up when the United States entered World War II and the federal government once again halted beverage alcohol production, this time so that distilleries could switch to 190-proof industrial alcohol for use in ammunition, plastics, antifreeze, and the like. After the war, Americans once again had money to spend, and distilleries cranked up production to provide them with bourbon to spend it on. The 1950s were a golden age of bourbon production in Kentucky. Distilleries started marketing their wares internationally. Special packaging became popular, notably the ceramic decanters sold by Jim Beam.

On May 4, 1964, Congress passed a resolution that declared bourbon whiskey to be "a distinctive product of the United States," just as Scotch whisky is distinctive to Scotland or Canadian whiskey to Canada. Then, as now, Kentucky was producing the lion's share of America's bourbon: by 1968, there were almost 9 million barrels of it aging in warehouses in the Bluegrass.

But the times were not the only things a-changin' in the late 1960s. So was the nation's drink of choice. And it wasn't bourbon.

"A DISTINCTIVE PRODUCT OF THE UNITED STATES"

In May 1964, Congress passed the following resolution declaring that bourbon whiskey could be produced only in the United States.

Whereas it has been the commercial policy of the United States to recognize marks of origin applicable to alcoholic beverages imported into the United States; and

Whereas such commercial policy has been implemented by the promulgation of appropriate regulations which, among other things, establish standards of identity for such imported alcoholic beverages; and

Whereas among the standards of identity which have been established are those for "Scotch whisky" as a distinctive product of Scotland, manufactured in Scotland in compliance with the laws of Great Britain regulating the manufacture of Scotch whisky for consumption in Great Britain and for "Canadian whisky" as a distinctive product of Canada manufactured in Canada in compliance with the laws of the Dominion of Canada regulating the manufacture of whisky for consumption in Canada and for "cognac" as grape brandy distilled in the Cognac region of France, which is entitled to be so designated by the laws and regulations of the French Government; and

Whereas "Bourbon whiskey" is a distinctive product of the United States and is unlike other types of alcoholic beverages, whether foreign or domestic; and

Whereas to be entitled to the designation "Bourbon whiskey" the product must conform to the highest standards and must be manufactured in accordance with the laws and regulations of the United States which prescribe a standard of identity for "Bourbon whiskey"; and

Whereas Bourbon whiskey has achieved recognition and acceptance throughout the world as a distinctive product of the United States: Now, therefore, be it

Resolved by the Senate (the House of Representatives concurring), That it is the sense of Congress that the recognition of Bourbon whiskey as a distinctive product of the United States be brought to the attention of the appropriate agencies of the United States Government toward the end that such agencies will take appropriate action to prohibit the importation into the United States of whisky designated as "Bourbon whiskey".

23

Big Names in Bourbon

Tracing the Kentucky bourbon family tree is a lot like looking up the bloodlines of Kentucky Derby winners: you'll encounter the same names time and again. Many families have worked in the distilling business for generations, partly because people born in Kentucky rarely leave, and the few who do usually have the good sense to come back.

One especially legendary name, of course, is Beam. Beams have been making whiskey in Kentucky ever since German immigrant Jacob Beam sold his first barrel in 1795. Seven subsequent generations have led what is today the Jim Beam Distillery. But Beams have also worked for just about every other major distillery in the state, and two descendants are currently reviving their branch's dormant legacy at a craft distillery they opened in 2011.

24

A bronze statue of Booker Noe, longtime Master Distiller at Jim Beam, keeps watch at the distillery. (Photo courtesy of the Kentucky Distillers' Association)

But first let's talk about the Jim Beam Distillery. Jacob Beam's son, David, eventually succeeded his father and expanded distribution. Three of David's four sons also worked in whiskey, but only one, David M. Beam, joined his father at the family company. During David M.'s tenure, he moved the distillery from Washington County to Nelson County to be closer to the railroad. David M. also had four sons, two of whom followed him into the company: James Beauregard "Jim" Beam (the famous one) and Park Beam.

The Beam distillery, like so many others, closed during Prohibition. After Repeal, Jim Beam rebuilt it in Clermont, Kentucky, its present location, as the Jim Beam Company. He had two children, T. Jeremiah and Margaret. Under T. Jeremiah's watch, the company opened a second distilling plant in 1954 near Boston, Kentucky. But because he had no children, it was his sister's son, Booker Noe, who became the sixth-generation distiller. He was initially Master Distiller at the Boston plant (now known as the Booker Noe plant), and eventually became a larger-than-life ambassador for the company. His son, Fred Noe, is the current Jim Beam Master Distiller. On May 2, 2016, Fred and his son, Freddie, the eighth generation of this bourbon-making family, filled the 14 millionth barrel of Jim Beam bourbon.

25

Heaven Hill Master Distillers Craig and the late Parker Beam (Photo courtesy of Heaven Hill)

THE FAMILY of BEAM

{ EST. 1760 }

Jacob Beam

David Beam

Joseph Beam

Minor Case Beam
M. C. Beam Distillery

Joseph "Mr. Joe" Beam
Stitzel-Weller Distillery &
Old Heaven Hill Springs Distillery

Guy

Walter

Jack
Barton Distillery

Paul
Limestone Branch
Distillery

Stephen
Limestone Branch
Distillery

Elmo
Maker's Mark
Distillery

Roy
Frankfort
Distillery

Wilmer
Taylor & Williams
Distillery

Desmond
Frankfort Distillery
& Master Distiller at
Old Kennebec Distillery

Charles
Seagram's Four Roses
Distillery

Roy
Frankfort
Distillery

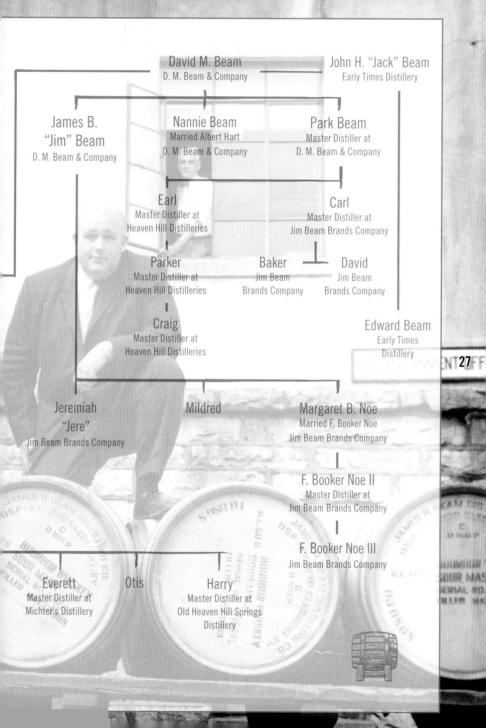

David M. Beam
D. M. Beam & Company

John H. "Jack" Beam
Early Times Distillery

James B. "Jim" Beam
D. M. Beam & Company

Nannie Beam
Married Albert Hart
D. M. Beam & Company

Park Beam
Master Distiller at
D. M. Beam & Company

Earl
Master Distiller at
Heaven Hill Distilleries

Carl
Master Distiller at
Jim Beam Brands Company

Parker
Master Distiller at
Heaven Hill Distilleries

Baker
Jim Beam
Brands Company

David
Jim Beam
Brands Company

Craig
Master Distiller at
Heaven Hill Distilleries

Edward Beam
Early Times
Distillery

Jeremiah "Jere"
Jim Beam Brands Company

Mildred

Margaret B. Noe
Married F. Booker Noe
Jim Beam Brands Company

F. Booker Noe II
Master Distiller at
Jim Beam Brands Company

F. Booker Noe III
Jim Beam Brands Company

Everett
Master Distiller at
Michter's Distillery

Otis

Harry
Master Distiller at
Old Heaven Hill Springs
Distillery

Now that you've wrapped your head around Noes distilling at Jim Beam, let's talk about the Beams distilling at Heaven Hill. David Beam's oldest son, Joseph M. Beam, had 14 children. One of them, Joseph L. "Joe" Beam, helped found the Heaven Hill distillery in Bardstown after Prohibition. Joe's son Harry Beam was Heaven Hill's first distiller; he was succeeded by Park Beam's son Earl, who left the Jim Beam Distillery for the job. Earl was followed by his son, Parker Beam (namesake of the distillery's annual Parker's Heritage Collection); Parker and his son, Craig, were co–Master Distillers

28

until Parker stepped down in 2012. (Parker passed away after a long battle with ALS in January 2017.) Craig Beam is now co–Master Distiller with Denny Potter. (Speaking of families, Heaven Hill is the largest independent family-owned and -operated producer and marketer of distilled spirits in the United States, having been owned by the Shapira family from the start.) Joe Beam and his other sons also worked at various times for Four Roses and for Maker's Mark.

Joseph M. Beam's oldest son, Minor Case Beam, owned a distillery in Nelson County in the early 1900s but sold it in 1910. He, his son, Guy, and his grandson Jack all worked at distilleries before and after Prohibition, but no one in that branch actually owned a distillery again until 2011, when Minor Beam's great-grandsons, Stephen and Paul Beam,

Paul *(left)* and Stephen Beam of Limestone Branch Distillery (Photo courtesy of the Kentucky Distillers' Association)

opened Limestone Branch in Lebanon, Kentucky. There, they honored the distilling heritage not only of their father's family but also of their mother's, the Dants, by resurrecting that family's most famous brand, Yellowstone Bourbon.

Finally, David Beam's youngest son, John "Jack" Beam, founded a distillery in Bardstown called Early Times. His son, Edward, was supposed to succeed him as distiller, but both men died in 1915. Brown-Forman eventually bought the brand name, and Early Times is still sold today.

In 2011, Rob Samuels became the eighth generation to lead his storied bourbon family when he took over as chief executive of Maker's Mark. The Samuels family has been in the whiskey business since 1840. Rob's grandparents, Bill and Margie Samuels, developed Maker's Mark, a smooth, sweet wheated bourbon, in the 1950s, and his father, Bill Samuels Jr., made the bourbon an international sensation through clever marketing.

Another father-and-son team has been making fine Kentucky bourbon for decades at Wild Turkey in Lawrenceburg, Kentucky. Master Distiller Jimmy Russell has worked at Wild Turkey for just over 60 years and has the longest tenure of any Master Distiller in the industry. His son, co–Master Distiller Eddie Russell, has been with Wild Turkey for "only" 35 years and jokingly introduces himself as "the new guy." Eddie's son Bruce entered the family business in 2015 as a brand ambassador for Russell's Reserve.

For members of these distilling dynasties, whiskey runs through the blood. They're not just making Kentucky bourbon. They're making Kentucky history.

29

Master Distillers Eddie *(left)* and Jimmy Russell of Wild Turkey (Photo courtesy of Wild Turkey)

2

Making Its Mark:
The Rise of
Premium Bourbon

"I think in 20 years we'll say 'a $5,000 bottle of bourbon' and no one will blink an eye. There is a shift happening right now . . . and I think nothing but good can come of it. It's sure better than the alternative, where you can't give the stuff away. We've seen that before."

—Harlen Wheatley, Master Distiller at Buffalo Trace Distillery

BY THE 1970s, bourbon producers were facing a big problem. They had 8.5 million barrels aging in warehouses across the state, but their amber spirit had fallen from favor. Young people, having rejected whiskey along with everything else the previous generation had preferred, were drinking lighter distilled spirits such as tequila and vodka along with beer and wine. Having failed to foresee this change when they made their sales predictions years in advance, distillers now had a glut of inventory that no one wanted.

And no one seemed to know how to turn things around.

"When I started at Brown-Forman 40 years ago, bourbon wasn't cool," says Chris Morris, now Master Distiller at the Louisville-based spirits company. "There were just the everyday brands: our flagship brand, Old Forester, and Early Times; our competitors, Old Grand-Dad, Old Crow,

Chris Morris, Master Distiller at Brown-Forman
(Photo courtesy of Brown-Forman)

Old Taylor, Old Fitzgerald. There was no activity in terms of excitement, no new brands, no annual Old Forester Birthday Bourbon. Everybody was fighting for the same pie, and the pie was shrinking."

With too much supply and not enough demand, some producers started cutting prices, but that just moved bourbon to the bottom shelf of the liquor store, and even lower in the public's estimation. The future looked dark indeed. Morris, who joined Brown-Forman in 1980, refers to this period as "the worst of times."

Today, instead of gathering dust in package stores, many bottles of bourbon never even make it to the shelves: they are deposited directly into the hands of eager customers. Regulars cruise the bourbon aisle at their favorite shops like sharks, looking for something new, and buying frenzies erupt when a hard-to-get brand like Pappy Van Winkle is released. Bourbon has become a hot collectible.

"All these limited editions are being hoarded by bourbon crazies who have bunkers full of juice," says Eric Gregory, president of the Kentucky Distillers' Association. "I don't know what bourbon apocalypse they are waiting for, but I love it!"

So what did distillers do to make bourbon cool again? They raised its profile—and they raised its price.

"Since the ending of Prohibition, as an industry, we've probably shot ourselves in the foot 10 times," Max Shapira, president of Heaven Hill

33

Heaven Hill's Max Shapira (Photo courtesy of Heaven Hill)

Distilleries, says in *Kentucky Bourbon Tales,* a project conducted by the University of Kentucky's Louie B. Nunn Center for Oral History and the KDA, in which I participated as an interviewer. "Then finally, we started to do some things right. We introduced single-barrels, small batches. Today, there is more innovation than you could ever possibly imagine— unique ages, alcohol proof levels, and mash bills; packaging and labeling; all the elements that go into attracting new consumers." Even flavored bourbon. "I mean, think about it: if someone in a marketing meeting even as little as five or six years ago had put his hand up and said, 'I think we need a cherry-flavored bourbon, or a honey-flavored one,' he would probably have been thrown out of the meeting. But these are the things that have helped to reinvent this segment of the industry."

And leading the way was a distillery in the middle of nowhere called Maker's Mark.

The first bottle of Maker's Mark Kentucky Straight Bourbon Whisky was filled in 1958 at Bill Samuels's distillery in tiny Loretto, Kentucky. At that point, many bourbon whiskeys were harsh and high proof—something you shot to feel the burn. Bill Samuels had a different idea. "He wanted to make a bourbon that actually tasted good," says his son, Bill Samuels Jr., chairman emeritus of Maker's Mark. To do that, he experimented with different grain combinations, eventually using red winter wheat in place of rye, which made his bourbon softer and sweeter.

{ *Just* A SIP }

As a general rule, whiskey *is spelled with an* e *in the United States and Ireland but without an* e *in Canada, Scotland, and Japan. Two notable exceptions are Maker's Mark Kentucky Straight Bourbon Whisky and Old Forester Kentucky Straight Bourbon Whisky.*

Bill Junior's mother, Margie Samuels, collected fine pewter. Each piece bore the mark of its maker, which was a sign of quality—so she suggested they call the new bourbon "Maker's Mark." She also designed the bottle and the label, including the font, and proposed that each bottle be sealed with red wax in the manner of expensive cognac. (Whenever Bill Senior

Maker's Mark Distillery, in the rolling hills of Marion County, Kentucky, was founded by Margie and Bill Samuels. (Photos courtesy of Beam Suntory)

objected to one of her suggestions for cost or other reasons, Bill Junior says, Margie would remind him who had graduated first in the class at the University of Louisville, and who had graduated last.)

Maker's Mark made its first profit in 1967: $1,000. The bourbon was popular in Kentucky but largely unknown outside the state. It would take a rocket scientist to launch it to national acclaim: Bill Samuels Jr., who joined the company in the early 1970s after a brief career in the aerospace industry. When he became president of Maker's Mark in 1975, he says, his father gave him one directive: "Don't screw up the whiskey."

Bill Junior didn't want to mess with the bourbon; he wanted more people to drink it. His father had always been reluctant to advertise. Bill Junior, on the other hand, has been known to wear a red suit that lights up to promote Maker's Mark. But in the beginning, he worked with the

Doe-Anderson agency in Louisville to develop two low-key approaches that his father could accept: establishing an informal group of "ambassadors," or Maker's Mark fans who were willing to talk up the brand and request that their favorite watering holes carry it; and creating a series of ads that read like letters to consumers and included the tagline, "It tastes expensive . . . and is." Doe-Anderson would later capitalize on Maker's Mark's red-wax seal in a series of clever billboards as the bottles became an industry icon, instantly recognizable on a back bar.

But none of it would have worked, Bill Samuels Jr. explains, if what was inside the bottle hadn't been good. "If we didn't have a product that people couldn't wait to go tell their friends about, then we were dead in the water, because there certainly wasn't any momentum for bourbon," he says. "And there was no such thing as 'premium' and 'super-premium' bourbon; it just didn't have any of the connoisseurs' cues. . . . If Maker's Mark was to become what we wanted it to become, after Dad took the shackles off a little bit, the reputation of bourbon had to change. And somebody had to be first."

In 1980, a reporter for *The Wall Street Journal* named David P. Garino made his way to Loretto. His resulting story, "Maker's Mark Goes Against the

36

Grain To Make Its Mark: Bourbon Distiller Is a Model of Inefficiency by Choice," ran on the front page. Suddenly, the distillery couldn't keep up with the demand for its bourbon.

Other distillers took note of the success that Maker's Mark was having by positioning its bourbon as special and sophisticated, and they followed suit. In 1984, Elmer T. Lee, distillery manager at George T. Stagg Distillery (now Buffalo Trace) in Frankfort, introduced the first bourbon that was mass-marketed as "single-barrel": Blanton's. Most bourbon is blended from the contents of many barrels in order to achieve a consistent taste profile. But now and again, distillers come across a single barrel that they think contains exceptional juice. Each bottle of bourbon labeled as

Blanton's single-barrel bourbon (Photo courtesy of Buffalo Trace Distillery)

single-barrel has been filled from just one of these so-called honey or sugar barrels.

{ *Just* A SIP }

Buffalo Trace's Elmer T. Lee Single Barrel Kentucky Straight Bourbon Whiskey was the drink of choice for Boyd Crowder, the antagonist in the Kentucky-set FX series Justified *(2010–2015).*

To consumers, the designation indicated a higher quality. It didn't hurt that single-barrel bourbon sounded a lot like the term "single-malt Scotch." Even though the terms don't mean the same thing (a single-malt Scotch is one produced in a single distillery), single-malt Scotches were beginning to fetch premium prices in the 1980s. Many more single-barrel bourbons would follow. In 1986, the creator was honored with his own label: Elmer T. Lee Single Barrel Kentucky Straight Bourbon Whiskey.

Near the end of the decade, Booker Noe, Master Distiller at Jim Beam, introduced another innovation: the small-batch bourbon. His Booker's, bottled at barrel strength with a label written in his own handwriting, was the first of what would become Beam's Small Batch Bourbon Collection; in 1992, it was joined by Baker's, Basil Hayden's, and Knob Creek, all marketed as ultrapremium bourbon whiskeys.

{ *Just* A SIP }

There is no official definition of, or requirement for, what constitutes a small-batch bourbon. A small batch can be drawn from one barrel or dozens of barrels—it means whatever the bottler wants it to mean.

To market these new high-end products, industry executives decided to send their distillers out to liquor stores and bars along with sales reps, both to educate the public about bourbon and to give the brands a personality.

Elmer T. Lee and Booker Noe went on the road, along with Jimmy Russell, who had become the head distiller at Wild Turkey in the late 1960s.

(Continued on page 42)

A LIMITED EDITION OF ONE: SINGLE-BARREL SELECTIONS

As the demand for limited-edition bourbon grows, many distilleries are now offering the most limited edition of all: a single barrel that is hand-picked by a liquor store, restaurant, or bar owner and bottled exclusively for that establishment.

Along with two other bourbon writers, Susan Reigler and Michael Veach, I have had the honor and privilege of participating in a number of these selections as a member of the Bourbon Board of Directors for Party Mart, an independently owned store in Louisville.

The procedure at most distilleries is very similar. We arrive at the tasting bar, usually located right in the barrel warehouse, where glasses, water, and crackers or chips have been arranged at each place. Three or four exceptional barrels, preselected by the Master Distiller, lie on their sides, bungs facing up. (Four Roses, which, with two mash bills and five yeast strains, has 10 recipes, pulls one of each.) The distiller, or a brand representative, removes the bung with a bung knocker and a chisel. Then, using a long copper "straw" called a whiskey thief, we take turns drawing bourbon from each barrel and depositing it either directly into the glasses or into a decanter that the distillery officials pour into the glasses.

38

The tasting room at Four Roses' warehouse and bottling facility (Photo: Carla Carlton)

We nose and taste each sample, taking notes on each and discussing our reactions. We are looking for superior bourbon, of course, but we are also on the hunt for a sample that has a taste profile that is distinctive in some way. Why would you pay extra for a single barrel of Old Forester that tastes exactly like Old Forester?

This exercise illustrates—dramatically in some cases—that no two barrels of bourbon are exactly alike, even barrels that were filled on the same day and aged for the same length of time right next to one another. Each one contains at least some dimension of its particular brand—the fruit note, maybe, or the spice—but not the entire spectrum. It's sort of like taking a step back from a bourbon and meeting its parents.

We first sample at barrel strength. If our selection will be gauged to the brand's usual proof for bottling (for example, 90 proof for Buffalo Trace), we then add a few drops of water and taste again. It's fascinating how this can alter the flavor; in a few cases, the addition of water has prompted us to change our selection. The winning barrel (or barrels) is marked, dumped, and bottled with either a special "private selection" label or tag attached (some with our names on them, which is pretty darned cool), then delivered to the store in a couple of months.

An entire barrel can cost anywhere from $5,000 to upwards of $15,000, depending on the distillery and the particular bourbon or whiskey purchased. The yield varies from barrel to barrel, but a good ballpark estimate is 150–250 bottles per barrel. The cost is worth it, Party Mart's Jerry Rogers says: "When you're in retail, you're selling the sizzle, not the steak. My Maker's Mark is the same as everyone else's. The single barrel program gives us the opportunity to do something different—something that separates us from everyone else."

Speaking of Maker's Mark, that distillery's new private barrel program, which began in November 2015, is unique. Rather than choosing a barrel, we "built" one. The program is designed to replicate the process that Bill Samuels Jr. followed to create Maker's 46, which spends an additional nine weeks in a barrel to which French oak staves have been added. In January 2016, when we traveled to Loretto, we were just the 20th group to participate. ➡

Over the course of several hours, we learned about how wood affects flavor by tasting samples that had aged in five types of finished oak, each accentuating a different note found in Maker's Mark: Baked American Pure 2, Seared French Cuvée, Maker's 46, Roasted French Mocha, and Toasted French Spice. Using round wooden chips representing the finishes and a board with 10 slots drilled into it, we came up with different barrel recipes, if you will, which the Maker's Mark folks created for tasting by adding those percentages to a graduated cylinder. Most groups create five to seven blends; we made six before choosing our winner: one Seared French Cuvée stave, three Maker's 46s, five Mochas, and one Toasted French Spice.

In the warehouse, a worker removed the head of a barrel and produced a large metal hoop onto which we hung our selected staves. The barrel was once again sealed; we signed it; and another employee filled it with mature Maker's. Several months later, the bottles arrived at Party Mart. Our Private Select had the smoothness of all Maker's Mark, but with a prominent chocolaty mocha flavor all its own. The board member who built it must have one great palate (she said modestly).

A Maker's Mark warehouse worker racks our signed Party Mart barrel to age for several more weeks. (Photo: Carla Carlton)

Maker's Mark Private Select (Photo courtesy of Beam Suntory)

(Continued from page 37)

Fred Noe, Booker Noe's son and the current Beam Master Distiller, refers to the trio as "the elder statesmen" of bourbon. "By being accessible, shaking hands, and telling the stories of the bourbon industry through their eyes, they laid the groundwork for the popularity of bourbon today," Fred says.

Jimmy Russell recalls stopping at a mom-and-pop liquor store in a small California town on his inaugural tour. For context, this would have been during the heyday of Bartles & Jaymes wine coolers, which advertised with actors playing the talkative Frank Bartles and the stone-faced Ed Jaymes. "There was an old gentleman sitting in the back in a rocking chair," Russell recalls. "We kept talking and going on, and he looked at me and said, 'You're real.' I said, 'What?' He said, 'Mama, come back here: this fella's real! He makes it!' I never will forget that."

Back then, it was a good day if a dozen people showed up for a free bourbon tasting. Nowadays, large events like *Whisky Advocate* magazine's four regional WhiskyFests, where VIP tickets go for up to $350 each, sell out months in advance. Aficionados are drawn by the opportunity to taste new and hard-to-get whiskeys, but an equal, if not larger, attraction is the chance to meet the Master Distillers of their favorite pours, who are now treated like rock stars of the whiskey world.

As an aside, there is no official definition of "Master Distiller"; it's a marketing term. Jim Rutledge, formerly of Four Roses, says he resisted using it—"distiller" was fine with him—until the marketing team finally wore him down. Charlie Downs of Heaven Hill's Evan Williams Bourbon Experience, who likens the role of Master Distiller to that of a head chef, says use of the term grew as distilleries did more public education and in-person promotion. "Putting a face with the product sells a lot of stuff."

So Jimmy Russell, who once flew around the country trying to persuade bars and package stores just to carry his Wild Turkey brands, now flies around the world to events where people stand in line to take a photo with him or get his autograph on a bottle. The longest-serving Master Distiller in the industry, he's a little stooped now, but don't think that 60-plus years at Wild Turkey has slowed him down much. A heavily tattooed bartender at Delilah's, a well-regarded bourbon bar in Chicago, described the energy that ran through the young crowd at a WhiskyFest after-party several years ago when a Town Car pulled up and Russell—who is often called "the Buddha of Bourbon"—stepped out. Patrons parted like the Red Sea as the legendary Master Distiller made his way to the upstairs bar to have a few more drinks. "That guy RULES!" the bartender said admiringly.

Bourbon innovation really took off in the 1990s, says Eric Gregory, president of the Kentucky Distillers' Association. "You had the creation of Woodford Reserve in 1996, Russell's Reserve . . . literally a bourbon for every palate. There was so much more diversity to choose from—and that catapulted the category to new heights." That innovation hasn't slowed a bit in the new century, with companies adding new expressions of their existing brands, such as Woodford Reserve Double Oaked, which is finished for nine months in a second barrel; Jim Beam Signature Craft, which is aged 12 years rather than the 4 years of Jim Beam White Label; and Old Forester Signature, a 100-proof version of the classic 86-proof Old Forester.

Dovetailing with this rise of bourbon was the resurgence of the cocktail, which got a bracing shot from the 1960s-era television series *Mad Men* and its suave, hard-drinking antihero, ad man Don Draper. In the very first scene of the premier episode, Don is seen scribbling an idea on a cocktail napkin. "Give me another one of these—an old-fashioned," he says to a passing waiter. All over the country, a new generation of bartenders—now called "mixologists"—has revived the old-fashioned, as well as other classic cocktails such as the Manhattan, the sidecar, and the julep, often crafting them with house-made syrups and infusions, as well as hand-chipped or molded ice. "It may take you 15 minutes to get a whiskey sour," Gregory says, "but it will be the best damned whiskey sour you've ever had in your whole life."

The cocktail craze has also driven the comeback of rye whiskey. With its spicy kick, rye holds its own against other flavors in a complex concoction, but that bold flavor is also what led to its downfall after Prohibition. The subcategory was much slower than bourbon to recover, but it's quickly making up for lost time. As recently as seven or eight years ago, there were only a handful of brands. Now, liquor stores devote entire sections of their shelf space to rye whiskeys. The increased demand caught some producers by surprise.

Wild Turkey had to put its Wild Turkey 101 Rye on hiatus in 2012 after supplies ran short, but they brought it back the following year. "We didn't know six or seven years ago that rye was going to do this," Master Distiller Russell says. "We can't turn the faucet on overnight."

{ *Just* A SIP }

The revival of classic cocktails has prompted a huge comeback in the rye whiskey category, which was almost nonexistent as recently as 2000. From 2009 through 2014, the volume of rye whiskey produced increased 536%, reaching more than a half-million cases, according to the Distilled Spirits Council of the United States, an industry group.

And, oh, yes—those flavored bourbons that Heaven Hill's Max Shapira referenced previously did come to pass. Wild Turkey actually released a honey-flavored liqueur in the late 1970s (it's now called American Honey), but the category didn't really start to take off until Jim Beam introduced Jim Beam Red Stag, a bourbon infused with black cherry flavor, in 2010. Now there are multiple bourbons flavored with cherry, apple, cinnamon, maple, and more—an attempt by the industry to lure younger drinkers. While the distillers obviously have to support their company's products, most of them will tell you off the record that they prefer their own bourbon straight, and they worry that the definition of bourbon is getting blurred.

A distiller who is vehemently *on* the record as opposing flavored bourbon is Jim Rutledge, who retired in 2015 as Master Distiller for Four Roses. That distillery has never produced a flavored bourbon, and he swears he will come back to haunt his successors if they ever do.

"I am so against these things because we're so good, as an industry. We don't need something [added]. But our industry has grown so fast, and is growing so fast, that you have people in corporate offices, financial people, thinking, 'Wow, here's a way we might be able to make more money,' " he told me shortly before he stepped down. "I always say, if somebody wants a blackberry-flavored bourbon, have your bartender mix it. Don't put it in the bottle. Number one, it's not bourbon, because under the law, the flavor of bourbon may not be adulterated. People were challenged when they first started doing some of these, and they said, 'We're not saying it's bourbon; we're saying it started out as bourbon. We're saying "four- or five-year-old Kentucky straight bourbon finished with artificial or natural fruit flavors." ' And daggone it, then, say what it is: a case of flavored Kentucky whiskey. Don't sacrifice the integrity, the credibility, the respect, the honesty of our industry that we've earned over the years.

"If we keep on allowing it, eventually anything that is brown-colored and alcohol and put in a bottle is going to be called bourbon. And it's getting there right now, and that's why I'm so against it. I love our industry."

Still, as an industry, that's a much nicer problem to have than worrying how to sell any bourbon at all—much less at some of the prices premium bourbon commands today. Twenty years ago, says Harlen Wheatley, Master Distiller at Buffalo Trace, "a 10-cent increase per bottle would hurt sales." Now, people form lines around liquor stores and participate in lotteries to buy Pappy Van Winkle, which is produced by his distillery, at whatever price retailers decide to charge.

"And the public is driving it, not us," he adds. "We still sell Pappy 23-year-old for $250, and that's what we suggest retailers sell it for, but it's a free market. What's a shame is that most Pappy 23 never hits the shelf. We're still shipping it out, but liquor-store owners are selling to preferred customers or buying it themselves."

Pappy Van Winkle and other coveted brands are also sold for astronomical sums (think four digits) on the secondary market, illegality notwithstanding. Pricing guides such as *Bourbon Blue Book* and *Bottle Blue Book* have been created in the past two years to help track sales and going rates. When empty Pappy Van Winkle bottles started being listed online for up to $200, it first appeared that collectors truly had gone mad—but those sales were quickly followed by warnings that counterfeiters were buying those bottles, refilling them with lesser juice, and then reselling them as the real thing, at suspiciously lower secondary prices. Bourbon buyer, beware.

Sometimes distributors ask why Buffalo Trace doesn't charge more for Pappy Van Winkle up front. While Wheatley certainly could, he says,

45

(Continued on page 49)

FOUR ROSES RISES AGAIN

No distillery better illustrates the up-and-down, then-up-again, story of bourbon than Four Roses, which quickly achieved national acclaim following its 1888 founding; nearly disappeared in the 1960s when its owner banished it overseas in favor of blended whiskey; and returned in the early 2000s to become one of the most respected brands in the business.

Founder Paul Jones Jr. initially elevated his distillery at least in part through outdoor advertising. He once rented space in New York City's Madison Square "for a sign of incandescent electric lights at a cost of twelve hundred dollars a month," longtime distillery manager and current brand ambassador Al Young writes in *Four Roses: The Return of a Whiskey Legend* (Butler Books, 2010).

Four Roses is said to be named in honor of Jones's successful request that a Southern belle signify her acceptance of his marriage proposal by wearing four roses to a dance. While Young can't say for sure that is accurate, what is certain is that after Jones's death, two of his nephews took over the Paul Jones Company business. One of them, Lawrence Jones, bought out the other and expanded the company into the Frankfort Distilling

Brent Elliott, Master Distiller at Four Roses
(Photo courtesy of Four Roses)

Company, which weathered Prohibition by receiving one of six licenses granted nationally to sell whiskey for medicinal purposes.

After Prohibition, Lawrence Jones built a new distillery in Louisville, which people called "Four Roses Distillery" after its most famous brand. Five years after Repeal, Four Roses had an animated neon sign in New York City's Times Square. It remained until the end of 1945 and can be seen in the background of Alfred Eisenstaedt's famous photo of a sailor kissing a nurse in celebration of the end of World War II. By the early 1950s, the Four Roses brand had name recognition on par with Coca-Cola, Ford, Jell-O, and Kodak, according to Young's book.

Capitalizing on this, Canadian company Seagram & Sons, which had acquired the distillery along with four others in Kentucky in the 1940s, officially changed the distillery's name to Four Roses Distilling Company in 1956. But Seagram was a blended-whiskey company, and with "light whiskey" rising in popularity in the United States, Seagram converted Four Roses to a blended whiskey as well.

Seagram's distillery in Lawrenceburg, Kentucky, was still making Four Roses Kentucky Straight Bourbon, but it was all being shipped to Europe and Japan. Not even the distillery workers could buy it.

The blended whiskey, meanwhile, which was not made in Kentucky, eventually included mostly grain-neutral spirits and became a cheap bottom-shelf product with a reputation as rotgut. "Seagram destroyed the name that Four Roses had built in the industry," says Jim Rutledge, who started working for the company in 1966. Rutledge was determined to bring it back.

After working for years in Louisville and New York, he requested a transfer to the Lawrenceburg distillery. In 1994, he became Master Distiller. He faced a huge challenge. Four Roses, the only Kentucky distillery that Seagram had retained, had steeply declined in quality. For three years, barrels produced there had averaged a quality rating of 1.9 out of 4. "Most of what was in the barrel inventory shouldn't have even been put away," Rutledge says. If the quality didn't turn around before June 1995, when the distillery shut down production for the summer, he was told, it would not reopen.

"From November through June, I doubt if I spent less than 16 hours a day in the distillery," he recalls. Every day, he knew, the distillery was

47

Jim Rutledge, Four Roses' former
Master Distiller (Photo: Carla Carlton)

getting better and better. Then, in the third week of February 1995, he got a call from the New York office. "Jim," a supervisor said, "what in the blankety-blank-blank are you guys *doing* down there, anyway?"

"My heart just dropped," Rutledge says. "I mean, I was absolutely, totally devastated. He went on and on, and then finally, he laughed and said, 'I'm just calling to let you know that you just received the first 4 you've had in more than three years.' I said, 'Why, you . . . ' "

Even so, Seagram denied Rutledge's continual requests to bring Four Roses bourbon back home. That didn't happen until 2002, when Japanese company Kirin, which had been marketing and distributing the bourbon in Japan since 1972, acquired all of Seagram's Four Roses holdings, including the proprietary yeast strains from each of the five US distilleries Seagram had once owned and its two mash bills. This gave Four Roses the 10 distinct bourbon recipes it still uses today—the most of any Kentucky distiller.

Kirin bought up as much of the blended whiskey as possible and removed it from the US market. Then a new Four Roses marketing plan was crafted, focusing on premium bourbon. In September 2004, Four Roses introduced its Single Barrel; two years later, it was the top-selling single barrel bourbon in Kentucky. In 2006, Four Roses introduced its Small Batch Bourbon, which was equally well received.

To commemorate Rutledge's 40th anniversary in the business, Four Roses issued a Limited Edition Single Barrel Bourbon in September 2007. The following year, a Limited Edition (LE) Small Batch was released; now an annual September release, it has won multiple industry awards. (Four Roses halted the annual release of the LE Single Barrel in 2015 when inventory ran low; however, it's still available through the distillery's Single Barrel Selection Program.)

The 2015 edition of the LE Small Batch was a tribute to Rutledge, who stepped down as Master Distiller in September of that year. The 2016 issue was the first to bear the signature of his successor, Brent Elliott.

Asked what he is most proud of in his long career, Rutledge doesn't hesitate: it was, he says, that six-month turnaround in quality at Four Roses in 1994–95 that saved the distillery and its employees.

"Seagram already had contracts ready to be signed with another distillery to start producing in the fall," he says. "But we had improved so much that corporate quality overruled corporate finance and said, 'We can't afford to lose this; it's too good.' If it wasn't for that, we wouldn't be having a conversation, and nobody would know Four Roses because it would have been long gone."

(Continued from page 45)

"I'm not worried about business this year. I'm worried about 30 years from now. If we gouge, will we be here then? If we are fair now, I think we'll be OK in 30 years."

But if prices continue to increase, he says, well, why not? "There are bottles of Scotch that sell for $50,000. People are willing to pay $5,000 for a bottle of wine. What's that—four drinks? Why wouldn't a good bottle of bourbon be worth that, too? People are realizing that bourbon is a good spirit, that you get quality for your money."

Ironically, the distiller that led the premium bourbon vanguard was among the last to expand its product line. For 50 years, Maker's Mark made one thing: Maker's Mark. But as he neared retirement as chairman, Bill Samuels Jr. began to consider his legacy—beyond not screwing up the whiskey. Starting with Maker's Mark, he, then–Master Distiller Kevin Smith, and Brad Boswell of Independent Stave, the cooperage that has made Maker's barrels since 1953, initiated a series of experimental barrels and finishes. The winning combination—No. 46—involved inserting 10 "seared" French oak staves into a new white-oak barrel, adding finished Maker's Mark, and aging the modified barrel in the coolest part of the warehouse for an additional 10 weeks.

The resulting bourbon, Maker's 46, which was released in 2010 in a slightly more elongated bottle sealed with the trademark red wax, has a bigger, bolder presence than original Maker's, but doesn't sacrifice any of its softness. It was followed by releases of Maker's Mark Cask Strength and Maker's 46 Cask Strength.

"I think if Dad were to come back today, he would be very pleased with how commercially successful Maker's has been and how we have managed not to screw the craft up along the way," Bill Junior says. "But I think he would be equally as thrilled with the reputation bourbon now has globally, and the wonderful job the other distilleries have done helping elevate this thing called bourbon."

THE THRILL OF THE HUNT

It's not just Pappy Van Winkle releases that have bourbon aficionados queueing up. Just about every major distiller now offers highly sought-after limited-edition bottlings. Here's a sampling:

Barton 1792

1792 LIMITED EDITIONS In the summer of 2015, Barton 1792 Distillery in Bardstown, which is owned by Sazerac, the parent company of Buffalo Trace, released the first-ever new expression of its Barton 1792: 1792 Sweet Wheat. That was followed in early 2016 by a limited-edition 1792 Single Barrel. More new expressions are planned.

(Photo courtesy of Buffalo Trace)

Brown-Forman

OLD FORESTER BIRTHDAY BOURBON Introduced in 2002, this bourbon is released annually on September 2, the birthday of Brown-Forman founder George Garvin Brown, and bottled in an 1800s-style decanter to commemorate the era when Old Forester was first produced.

OLD FORESTER WHISKEY ROW SERIES So far there have been three entries in this series, which attempts to re-create the flavors of earlier versions of Old Forester. The first, 1870 Original Batch, released in 2014, was blended from whiskey in three different warehouses, because the original bourbon was a blend of whiskey purchased from three different distillers. The second, Old Forester 1897 Bottled in Bond (2015), honors the federal Bottled-in-Bond Act of 1897, which declared that whiskey had to be the product of one distillation season, of one distiller, and from one distillery; aged in a federally bonded warehouse for at least four years; and bottled at full 100 proof. Old Forester 1920 Prohibition Style (2016) celebrates the brand's continued production during Prohibition under one of 10 permits for "medicinal" whiskey.

WOODFORD RESERVE DISTILLERY SERIES The newest of the distillery's special lines, this series, begun in 2015, has featured Double Double Oaked, Sweet Mash Redux, and Frosty Four Wood.

WOODFORD RESERVE KENTUCKY DERBY COMMEMORATIVE As the Official Bourbon of the Kentucky Derby, Woodford Reserve releases a special 1-liter bottle in March featuring artwork by noted equine artists.

WOODFORD RESERVE MASTER'S COLLECTION There have been 10 releases in this series, which has produced a variety of whiskeys, including a rye and a double-malt selection, since its initial Four Grain Bourbon in 2006. The most recent, in 2015, was 1838 Style White Corn.

51

(Photo courtesy of Brown-Forman)

Buffalo Trace

ANTIQUE COLLECTION Since 2000, collectors have tracked this annual release of five limited-edition whiskeys: George T. Stagg, William Larue Weller, Thomas H. Handy Sazerac Rye, Eagle Rare (17 Years Old), and Sazerac Rye (18 Years Old).

EXPERIMENTAL COLLECTION Buffalo Trace has released more than 20 spirits since 2006 under this label, the results of various experiments with factors such as mash bills, types of barrel staves, and finishing techniques. In 2015, Buffalo Trace completed its most ambitious experimental effort, the Single Oak Project. The distillery selected 96 oak trees in

(Photo courtesy of Buffalo Trace)

the Missouri Ozarks with different grain profiles. Each tree was divided into two parts, top and bottom, and a single barrel was made from each section. Each of those 192 barrels was filled with either wheat- or rye-recipe bourbon at two different proofs, and they were housed in two different warehouses—seven variables in all. The 192 bottlings were aged for eight years, then released incrementally, with enthusiasts voting on their favorites online. The winning bourbon (Barrel #80) was a rye recipe, entered into a barrel made from oak harvested from the bottom half of the tree. Mark Brown, president and CEO of Sazerac, which owns Buffalo Trace, jokes that soon "you'll go into the forest and see all these trees just kind of hanging there with the bottoms cut out."

Four Roses

FOUR ROSES LIMITED EDITION SMALL BATCH Released annually in September for Bourbon Heritage Month, this blend from several select barrels was named American Whiskey of the Year by *Whisky Advocate* magazine in both 2012 and 2013.

(Photo courtesy of Four Roses)

Heaven Hill

PARKER'S HERITAGE COLLECTION This annual collection, first produced in 2006, honors the late Parker Beam, Heaven Hill Master Distiller Emeritus, and has featured a Kentucky straight-malt whiskey, a wheat whiskey, a 27-year-old bourbon, and a bourbon finished in cognac. After Parker Beam was diagnosed with amyotrophic lateral sclerosis several years ago, part of the proceeds from the collection has gone toward ALS research and treatment.

(Photo courtesy of Heaven Hill)

Jim Beam

DISTILLER'S MASTERPIECE Billed as the "best of the best," this extra-aged Kentucky Straight Bourbon Whiskey has been barrel-finished in Pedro Ximénez sherry casks.

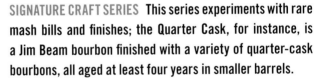

BOOKER'S BOURBON Booker's batches of bourbons are special releases that come out several times each year, with one-of-a-kind labels and a name that reflects an aspect of the life of Booker Noe, longtime Beam Master Distiller.

SIGNATURE CRAFT SERIES This series experiments with rare mash bills and finishes; the Quarter Cask, for instance, is a Jim Beam bourbon finished with a variety of quarter-cask bourbons, all aged at least four years in smaller barrels.

(Photo courtesy of Beam Suntory)

Wild Turkey

THIS LEGENDARY BOURBON BRAND features several over-aged expressions of Wild Turkey, including Diamond Anniversary, Master's Keep, and Tradition.

(Photo courtesy of Wild Turkey)

53

From Mash to Masterpiece: How Bourbon Is Made

"Bourbon is easy to understand.
It tastes like a warm summer day."

—*Deputy US Marshal Raylan Givens (Timothy Olyphant), FX's* Justified

56

SO WHAT EXACTLY *IS* this thing called bourbon? Even if you're
a beginning enthusiast, you've probably heard that all bourbon is whiskey,
but not all whiskey is bourbon. That's catchy, and true, but it doesn't
explain anything. As with so many things, the devil is in the details.

Whiskey, by the most basic definition, is a distilled spirit made from
grain—as opposed to fruit (wine), agave (tequila), or juniper berries (gin).
Bourbon, therefore, is a whiskey. But unlike other whiskeys, bourbon must
meet additional standards that have been established by the US government. These rules are listed in the Code of Federal Regulations, 27 5.22:
The Standards of Identity. Bourbon, in fact, is one of the most regulated
alcoholic spirits in the world.

There are three main differences between bourbon whiskey and other
types of whiskey:

First, the type and the amount of grain are specified. While whiskey
can be made from any grain, such as barley, wheat, or rye—I've even sampled
a nutty quinoa whiskey at Corsair Distillery in Bowling Green, Kentucky—
bourbon must begin with a grain mixture that is at least 51% corn.

Second, bourbon must be aged in a brand-new charred-oak vessel. That's right: a barrel may be used only one time to make bourbon.

Finally, unlike distillers of other types of whiskeys, bourbon distillers are forbidden to add any coloring or flavoring to their product. The only thing that can be added is water.

In addition, bourbon must be distilled to no more than 160 proof (80% alcohol by volume); must enter the barrel at no more than 125 proof (62.5% ABV); and, like all whiskeys, must be bottled at no less than 80 proof (40% ABV).

How long does bourbon have to age? The answer might win you a bar bet: there is no minimum aging requirement. More than once, I've heard Jimmy Russell, longtime Master Distiller at Wild Turkey, say, "You could take whiskey off the still at 120 proof, pour it into an oak bucket that's been charred on the inside, funnel it into a bottle, and you'd have bourbon." It wouldn't be very good bourbon, however, because aging is an essential component of the bourbon-making process. More about that in a bit.

Bourbon that meets all of the requirements above and has been aged for at least two years may be called "straight" bourbon (but doesn't have to be). Until bourbon is four years old, its age must be listed on the label. After that, distillers don't have to list the age, but many do, because older bourbons have more cachet with consumers (see Pappy Van Winkle Family Reserve 23-Year). If a bourbon is blended from different batches, the age statement must be the age of the youngest bourbon in the blend. And if you want to call your bourbon "Kentucky bourbon," it must be distilled in the state of Kentucky.

57

{ *Just* A SIP }

If the label on a bottle says "Kentucky straight bourbon," the spirit was made in Kentucky and is at least two years old. If it doesn't have an age statement beyond that, it's at least four years old, and probably somewhere between four and eight. Once bourbon gets to be older than eight, most distillers will note that on the label.

But let's get back to what's inside the bottle. As I'm sure you've discovered, not all bourbon brands taste the same—not by a long shot. Some are sweet, others are spicy, and the flavor profiles cover a wide spectrum, from nutty to fruity to floral. If all bourbon must be made following the same rules, and all distillers use essentially the same process, how is it possible to produce such different taste profiles? At every step of bourbon production, distillers have choices to make, and it is those choices that determine the flavors you find in your Glencairn glass.

Grain

The first decision a distiller must make in crafting a bourbon is the **mash bill,** or grain recipe. While the law says that recipe must contain a minimum of 51% corn, distillers are free to play with the other 49%. Most of them use more than the minimum amount of corn—more like 60%–75%—and a combination of rye and malted barley for the balance.

In a few notable bourbon brands, wheat is substituted for rye. You've probably heard of at least two of them: Pappy Van Winkle and Maker's Mark; others include W. L. Weller (Buffalo Trace) and Larceny (Heaven Hill). When a distiller uses wheat rather than rye, the result is called a wheated bourbon, or a "wheater." To imagine the difference, think about the taste of rye bread versus wheat bread—the former is spicier, while the latter is softer and sweeter. Heaven Hill also produces Bernheim Original Kentucky Straight Wheat Whiskey, which has a mash bill of 51% soft

Grain display at
Corsair Distillery
(Photo: Carla Carlton)

New Riff Distilling's 60-foot-tall copper still
(Photo: Carla Carlton)

winter wheat with a balance of corn and barley. (By the same token, rye whiskey must be made from a recipe that is at least 51% rye.)

While some distillers guard their mash bills as zealously as Kentucky Fried Chicken's Harland Sanders guarded his 11 secret herbs and spices, others are happy to provide them. Remember: the grain recipe is just one source of a bourbon's flavor profile. Knowing that a particular mash bill is X% corn, Y% rye, and Z% barley gives you only part of the equation.

One distillery willing to share is New Riff Distillery in Newport, Kentucky, across the Ohio River from Cincinnati. On a tour of this craft distillery, which opened in May 2014, you learn that New Riff's bourbon mash bill is 75% corn, 20% rye, and 5% malted barley. New Riff also notes that its corn is sourced from the Charles Fogg farm in Decatur County, Indiana. Most distillers use locally grown grains when possible, and once they find a good source, they tend to stick with it.

{ *Just* A SIP }

In keeping with the popular farm-to-table movement, many craft distilleries, such as MB Roland in Pembroke, Kentucky, grow their own grains and promote their products as "grain to glass." But larger distilleries are experimenting, too. In 2015, Buffalo Trace, for instance, began planting non-GMO corn, rye, and barley on 18 acres of its holdings in Frankfort, Kentucky, which will be used to make "single estate" bourbon.

In any case, once the desired grains have been inspected for quality, they are milled into a powder and added to a **mash tub,** or cooker. It's there that the second source of flavor is added.

Water

Just as water is essential to life, it is a key ingredient in bourbon. That's why you will find all distilleries built near an abundant source of it. Kentucky is particularly blessed with this resource; the state has some 90,000 miles of streams, according to the Kentucky Geological Survey. But it's not just the amount of running water that is important to bourbon production in Kentucky. It's what that water is running through: limestone.

Kentucky sits atop a limestone aquifer. This sedimentary rock is relatively soft, giving much of the Commonwealth what is known as karst topography—terrain formed as groundwater dissolved bedrock. That's why Kentucky has an abundance of caves, including the world's longest known cave system, the aptly named Mammoth Cave. That's also why eight classic Corvettes were damaged or destroyed in February 2014 when a 30-foot-deep sinkhole opened up underneath the National Corvette Museum in Bowling Green, about 27 miles southwest of Mammoth Cave.

So, OK, limestone isn't always a good thing. But when it comes to water, limestone acts as a natural filter, removing harsh elements like iron that you would not want in your glass (mainly because they would turn the bourbon black). Limestone also adds calcium carbonate, which helps during the next step, fermentation.

{ *Just* A SIP }

Kentucky's calcium-rich water is commonly cited as a factor in producing the state's champion Thoroughbred horses. I can't vouch for that, but if you want to claim that you drink Kentucky bourbon because it's good for your teeth and bones, you go right ahead.

During the grain mixture's time in the mash tub, the starch in the grains is broken down into simple sugars. Most large Kentucky distillers also add what's called **setback** (or, alternatively and somewhat confusingly, **backset**) to the mash—a portion of the spent mash from the previous distillation. The setback, added to ensure consistency from batch to batch, lowers the pH of the new mash. Whiskey produced this way is known as **sour mash.** (Conversely, whiskey that doesn't use setback is known as **sweet mash.**) To go back to the bread analogy, think of sourdough bread, which begins with a starter made from flour, water, and, as with bourbon, yeast.

Fermentation

After the mash is cooked, it goes into another large tub called the **fermenter,** which is made of stainless steel or cypress. The distiller cools the mash, typically by running cold water through pipes spiraling down around the inside of the fermenter, and then adds yeast. The yeast begins to feed on those simple sugars in the mash, converting them to carbon dioxide and alcohol. Bubbles of CO_2 rise to the top and burst on the

61

Mash is pumped into a fermenter at Town Branch Distillery in Lexington, Kentucky. (Photo: Clay Carlton)

Bubbles break on the surface in this fermenter at Woodford Reserve Distillery in Versailles, Kentucky, as yeast converts sugars in the mash into carbon dioxide and alcohol. (Photo courtesy of Brown-Forman)

surface. An active fermenter is like a boiling cauldron, except there's no fire underneath: all of the shimmering heat comes from the chemical reaction taking place.

{ *Just* A SIP }

Some distilleries, such as Woodford Reserve in Versailles, Kentucky, where the mash is fermented in 7,500-gallon cypress tanks, will let you dip your finger into the roiling mash while you're on a tour and taste the tangy, slightly grainy liquid. (This is not, however, considered adding flavor.)

Each distillery uses its own proprietary yeast strain, and if you think distillers are cagey about their mash bills, try getting them to tell you anything about their yeast. They guard that information as zealously as they protect the fungus itself. Yeast is a living thing, after all. It can quickly mutate, and if it gets too hot, it dies. "We keep it stored around everywhere," says Jimmy Russell, the legendary Master Distiller at Wild Turkey. Both Jimmy and his son, co–Master Distiller Eddie Russell, keep Wild Turkey yeast in their refrigerators at home in case something happens to the batch at the distillery. The survival of the yeast is a big deal, because most large distilleries have been using the same strains for decades.

"We're still using the same strain of yeast in our company as when I came here," says Jimmy, who celebrated his 60th year at Wild Turkey in 2014. Similarly, the Jim Beam distillery has been using the same yeast strain for more than 75 years, since the end of Prohibition. Four Roses Distillery has five different yeast strains, one each from five Kentucky distilleries that were once owned by its former parent company, Seagram, before it sold all but the current Lawrenceburg, Kentucky, location. When married to the distillery's two mash bills, these strains give Four Roses 10 distinct bourbon recipes, the most of any Kentucky distillery.

Once the yeast has gobbled up all the sugar and the liquid in the fermenter has calmed, the mash is known as **wash** or **distiller's beer,** and it indeed smells and tastes like light beer. Turning that beer into bourbon doesn't require a miracle, however—just another scientific process.

63

{ *Just* A SIP }

Would-be moonshiners: this is a good time to note that unlike home brewing, which is legal, home distilling is a felony. It's also considerably more dangerous. Wort for beer might scorch or boil over on the stove. Whiskey can explode.

Distillation

During distillation, the alcohol in the distiller's beer is isolated and captured during a process that transforms it from a liquid into a gas, and then back into a liquid. Two types of stills are used to make bourbon: the **column still** and the **pot still.**

The Column Still

As its name implies, a column still is round—as much as 3–5 feet in diameter—and usually several stories tall. Patented in 1831 by the Irish inventor Aeneas Coffey, the column still is the most common type used by large distilleries because it can make a great quantity of alcohol in a single run (which is why it's also known as a **continuous still**).

Column stills are fitted inside with a series of horizontal plates. The distiller's beer is pumped into the column from near the top and flows across each plate in turn, cascading to the bottom. At the same time, steam is injected from the bottom. Because the boiling point of alcohol is lower than that of water, the alcohol vaporizes and travels upward, where it's captured and condensed, while water and any solids left from the grain continue their downward journey.

The Pot Still

Rounder and squatter than a column still, a pot still looks like, well, a pot. Because spent grain has to be removed from a pot still, it can be used for just one batch at a time. Heat is applied to the bottom of the pot still to vaporize the alcohol, which then flows through a condensing coil, where it is cooled back into liquid form.

Copper stills at Wilderness Trail Distillery (Photo courtesy of the Kentucky Distillers' Association)

{ *Just* A SIP }

Pot stills are more commonly associated with Scotch malt whisky and Irish whiskey. In the United States, they're mainly used by smaller craft distillers, with one key exception: Woodford Reserve, which is triple-distilled in Versailles, Kentucky. The distillery's three copper pot stills are the highlight of a tour of Woodford Reserve, and their image is stamped onto every barrelhead.

Most stills are made of copper. In addition to being an excellent conductor of heat, copper reacts with unwanted sulfur compounds in distiller's beer and removes them. Copper stills are also beautiful. Polished to a glowing sheen, they are often the centerpiece of a distillery, both from an aesthetic and a production standpoint.

Some distillers let the copper oxidize, taking on an interesting patina. "Over the years, our still went from looking like a shiny new penny to—well, it's kind of like a mood ring, you know?" says Pat Heist, co-owner of Wilderness Trail Distillery in Danville, Kentucky. "On any given day, depending on what we're doing and the temperature we're running it, it might turn purple."

Whether a distiller is using a column still or a pot still, the process of distillation is the same. As the temperature of the solution inside the still increases, compounds—or congeners—in the alcohol start to volatilize, or turn to vapor. About the first 5% to vaporize is captured and discarded. Called the "heads," it's made up of lethal compounds such as methanol. (If you've heard the saying that drinking moonshine will make you go blind, that's because during Prohibition, some moonshiners bottled everything that came off the still—including methanol.)

Once the alcohol reaches the proof and taste profile the distiller is looking for, it's known as the "hearts." This ethyl alcohol is what is captured to be barreled. At the end of the run, the distiller separately collects the "tails." This low-proof liquid still contains ethyl alcohol, but also has compounds such as propanol, which would give the bourbon an oily mouthfeel. The tails will be recycled in a later distillation to capture the remaining ethyl alcohol.

Most bourbon distillers run the hearts through a second distillation in a smaller still, known as a doubler or a thumper, to further refine the spirit. The more congeners that are stripped from the alcohol, the less flavor the distillate itself will have. As for the leftover, or "spent," mash, distillers often sell it to local farmers as silage for cattle or hogs. (The more delicate stomachs of horses can't handle it.) They have the happiest cows in the county, they'll tell you.

Maturation

Many people are surprised to learn that when bourbon comes off the still, it is as clear as vodka. Called **new make,** or, more colorfully, "white dog,"

Top: Brown-Forman coopers hand-select 33 staves for each barrel; *bottom:* a worker prepares barrels for the warehouse at Buffalo Trace. (Photos: Top, courtesy of the Kentucky Department of Travel; bottom, Chad Carlton)

it tastes at this point mostly like its majority ingredient, corn. So how does bourbon achieve all of those other flavors and that wonderful amber color?

Makers of some spirits are allowed to add flavorings and caramel coloring. "Some rums and different things, they literally are just a bunch of flavor components put together with grain spirit alcohol in there," Heist says. "It's freaking gross."

Under federal law, however, nothing but water may be added to bourbon. Up to 75% of bourbon's flavor, and 100% of its color, comes from the barrel, picked up by the distillate as it expands and contracts into the wood over time. The barrel, therefore, isn't just a container: it's an important ingredient in the bourbon recipe. And again, distillers have some options that will affect the flavor of the bourbon that is dumped from those barrels.

Bourbon must be aged in brand-new oak barrels that have been charred on the inside. While the type of oak isn't specified, most bourbon barrels are made of white oak, because it contains a substance called tylosis that allows it to retain liquid. Before barrel staves are cut, the lumber is air-dried, or "seasoned," which reduces both the water content of the wood and its tannins, which add bitterness to bourbon. The lumber is air-dried for at least six months, but a distiller might choose to season it for several years—or to further season the staves themselves.

Distillers also specify how long and at what temperature they want their barrels toasted and charred. Each process serves a different purpose.

During toasting, the insides of the barrels are heated to a specific temperature. The heat breaks down chemical bonds in the wood, releasing molecules (such as vanillin) that add flavor, and caramelizes its sugars, which provide not just flavor but bourbon's characteristic amber color.

During charring, the insides of the barrels are blasted with higher heat for a much shorter period of time. This blisters the surface of the wood into charcoal, which acts as a filter as the bourbon expands and contracts, mellowing the bourbon's flavor. The levels of char range from one to four. A No. 4 char, the deepest, is also known as "alligator char," because the wood's crackled surface resembles the leathery skin of an alligator.

Most distilleries use poplar bungs, or stoppers, in their barrels, because poplar expands when wet and forms a tight seal. Maker's Mark uses walnut bungs; because the distillery ages not to a certain number of years, but "to taste," the barrels are tapped more frequently and the walnut bungs are less likely to splinter.

{ *Just* A SIP }

A standard bourbon barrel weighs between 90 and 120 pounds. When filled with 53 gallons of bourbon, it weighs between 500 and 515 pounds (or about half the weight of a full-grown Thoroughbred). That's far too heavy for one person to lift, of course. But when a barrel is on its side, one person can easily roll it using just one hand.

Warehouses

After the barrels are filled, they are placed in a warehouse (often called a **rickhouse,** after the ricks, or open shelves, that hold the barrels), where they remain for anywhere from 2 years to up to 23 or more. You'll sometimes hear people say the barrels are resting, or slumbering. That's not quite true, though: while the barrels themselves may not be moving, what's inside them definitely is.

As the seasons change, so does the bourbon. In the heat of summer, the liquid expands and is forced into the wood, where the alcohol content dissolves the caramels and sugars in the toasted wood. As the temperature becomes colder, the liquid contracts, bringing those flavors with it while losing undesirable harshness through the filtering effect of the char.

The type of warehouse and a barrel's position within it are yet more factors that can influence the taste of the final product.

Not all warehouses are built from the same materials. Some are brick or stone (those at Woodford Reserve and Buffalo Trace, for instance); others are wood or metal-clad wood (such as those at Wild Turkey). Some rickhouses have wood floors; others have concrete floors. Some have windows, some don't. Alone among major Kentucky distillers, Four Roses ages its bourbon in single-story warehouses, reasoning that this allows the barrels to age more uniformly.

In a multistory rickhouse, barrels stored on higher floors, or "at the top of the house," typically experience higher temperatures, and therefore greater rates of evaporation. This is called "the angels' share," and it's what makes a

69

A warehouse, also known as a rickhouse, at Willett Distillery in Bardstown, Kentucky (Photo courtesy of the Kentucky Distillers' Association)

BONDED WAREHOUSE C

70

bourbon warehouse smell like heaven. Because most of what is evaporating is water, the bourbon in these barrels tends to be more concentrated and will usually have a higher proof than the bourbon in barrels at lower levels.

That's not always the case, however. I once participated in a tasting at Heaven Hill in Bardstown, Kentucky, that compared the contents of a barrel on the topmost floor of a seven-story warehouse with the bourbon in barrels on the fourth and first floors. All of the barrels had been aging for 10 years. As expected, the bourbon from the seventh floor had the highest proof: 133.2. The juice on the fourth floor measured 125.3. Then distiller Charlie Downs drew a sample from the barrel on the first floor. It was 127.4 proof—higher than that on the fourth.

Even barrels that were filled with bourbon from the same batch on the same day and aged for the same amount of time right next to each other can differ in proof and flavor. "There could be subtle differences in the pigments of the staves," says Nancy Fraley, who does custom blending and sensory analysis for distillers. "Even in a barrel made from a single tree, the south side of that tree will grow much differently than the north side will. But most barrels don't come from just one tree, so now you have all these staves from many different kinds of conditions. A few staves might have tighter grains, or some might have a coarse grain. You get that into a bunch of barrels, you're bound to have a number of different conditions going on."

Rotating the barrels, or periodically moving them from one place in a warehouse to another, is one way to ensure more consistency, but for large distillers whose warehouses hold hundreds of thousands of barrels, that is no longer practical. In this case, distillers periodically taste the bourbon in various locations and maintain their brands' signature flavor by combining bourbon from multiple barrels.

{ *Just* A SIP }

Maker's Mark is the only major distiller in Kentucky that still rotates its barrels.

The majority of distillers in Kentucky leave the temperature variations to Mother Nature. Brown-Forman, on the other hand, uses a process called heat cycling in its warehouses, which are made of brick and have few windows. Essentially, the distillery can put its barrels through several "winters" and "summers" per year. Brown-Forman conducts single barrel selections of Old Forester at a tasting bar inside Warehouse L. This can lead to what is literally a breathtaking experience when a tasting falls during a heat cycle in the summer. During one such adventure, the angels' share made my eyes water the moment I stepped inside, and putting my nose into the tasting glass, which would normally burn, felt like strapping on an oxygen mask.

"Welcome to the Old Forester Inferno," said Master Distiller Chris Morris.

 ## BUFFALO TRACE'S WAREHOUSE X

On a gentle hill at Buffalo Trace, just above the main distillery buildings and just below the home that Col. Albert Blanton built for his bride in 1934, stands a little brick warehouse. At 30 by 50 feet, it holds just 150 barrels—a fraction of the 25,000 barrels in a typical Buffalo Trace warehouse.

The building may be small, but there's a big idea behind it: inside its appropriately mysterious-sounding Warehouse X, the distillery in Frankfort, Kentucky, may very well discover the secret to making the perfect bourbon.

Built in 2013 at a cost of $1 million, Warehouse X is essentially five warehouses in one. Four of its five chambers can be sealed, with their temperature and humidity independently controlled by laboratory-grade

Warehouse X
(Photo: Chad Carlton)

HVAC systems. A fifth chamber, which runs down the center of the warehouse, is under roof but otherwise open to the elements. Barrels in this chamber, called "the breezeway," age naturally.

"The whiskey in those barrels has been exposed to temperatures ranging from 105 degrees Fahrenheit to negative 10," Master Distiller Harlen Wheatley says, pointing out their rusted hoops. "There is not another barrel in the world that has experienced that."

Experiments conducted in Warehouse X allow Wheatley to explore how temperature, light, airflow, and humidity affect barrels and the liquid inside them. When it comes to bourbon, "I don't like surprises, and I like to know why," says the distiller, who holds degrees in chemistry and chemical engineering. Why, for instance, do barrels from certain floors of a rickhouse tend to taste better? Is the common belief that bourbon ages better in barrels near a window true? "We're fixin' to find out."

In the summer of 2015, the barrels were halfway through a two-year experiment on the effects of light. Chamber One was operating at 50% light, with the temperature and humidity mimicking those affecting the control barrels in the breezeway. The barrels in Chambers Two and Three were being kept in total darkness, but while the temperature and humidity in Chamber Two remained constant, those factors in Chamber Three were also following the variations in the breezeway. In Chamber Four, the barrels were also experiencing the temperature and humidity of the control barrels, but the lights were being kept on at all times. The chambers can be viewed on computer screens in the breezeway.

"Already, in 12 months, we are learning things no one else in the world knows," Wheatley says. "At the end of this, we will have thousands of data points, and we will be able to attach that data to tastings. So if something is really good, we'll be able to say, 'Well, duh. That was aged at 40% humidity,' or whatever."

Buffalo Trace is widely known for its experimental program, which began with 1 barrel in 1989 and has grown to more than 4,000 barrels today. Through the years, variables tested have included recipes, types of barrels, and finishes, among others.

But while other distilleries have researched barrels and bourbon, no one has researched how the structure of a warehouse affects bourbon, says Mark Brown, president and CEO of Sazerac, which owns Buffalo Trace. The insights gained from Warehouse X will "hopefully put us one step closer to producing the perfect bourbon."

Wheatley may choose to publicize a few of those insights, but most of his findings will remain proprietary. "Of course, when we build our next warehouse and it's all windows," he jokes, "you might be able to make a good guess."

Bottling

Once a distiller has determined that the bourbon is ready, the barrels are dumped for bottling in the gauging room. Most have their contents filtered to remove bits of char. If a bourbon is destined to be a single-barrel selection, its entire contents are bottled at barrel strength, with no water added. Otherwise, the bourbon is **gauged,** or gets water added to bring its proof down to the desired level. It's then pumped to the bottling line.

Most bottling lines in large distilleries are automated. A machine rinses the empty bottles with bourbon, rather than water, so the proof isn't altered. The bottles are then filled, sealed, and labeled. Some brands, such as Blanton's, are labeled by hand. At Maker's Mark, bottles are hand-dipped in signature red wax.

As noted above, a dumped barrel cannot be used again to make bourbon. But it can be used for other types of whiskey. Even after it's emptied, the typical bourbon barrel still carries several gallons of bourbon within its walls—enough to add flavor and smoothness to a secondary spirit. Many bourbon barrels are shipped to Scotland for aging Scotch whisky; an increasing number of craft brewers are also using bourbon barrels to finish their ales.

A Maker's Mark worker can hand-dip 23 bottles in red wax per minute. (Photo courtesy of Beam Suntory)

Unlike wine, whiskey does not continue to age in the bottle. Unless the seal has been broken and the contents allowed to oxidize, a bottle of bourbon filled in 1973 should still taste the same today. Once you've opened a bottle, the bourbon will remain drinkable for years, especially if you keep it at least half full, which will slow evaporation—at least, that's what I'm told. I've never had a bottle last that long.

{ *Just* A SIP }

Each batch of bourbon at New Riff Distillery in Newport, Kentucky, uses enough corn for 69,372 bags of popcorn and an amount of rye that weighs as much as a walrus.

 ## ROLL OUT THE BARREL

Brown-Forman, the only major spirits company to own and operate a cooperage, celebrated the 70th anniversary of its barrel-making facility in Louisville, Kentucky, in February 2016. The cooperage makes about 600,000 barrels per year—almost 1 per minute—for its brands including Woodford Reserve, Old Forester, Early Times, and Canadian Mist. To keep up with demand for Jack Daniel's, its Tennessee whiskey, Brown-Forman opened a second cooperage in Decatur, Alabama, in July 2014 to craft barrels exclusively for that spirit. ➡

75

Barrel charring at Brown-Forman cooperage
(Photo: Carla Carlton)

While each brand's barrels are made to its own recipe, the overall process is the same. Seasoned oak is first cut into wide and narrow pieces, and short and long pieces. All of the pieces are planed smooth. The short ones are fitted together with wooden pegs and cut into a circle to form barrelheads, while the long pieces are milled into staves—wider in the middle than at the ends to allow for the curve of the barrel.

Workers hand-fit 31–33 staves, both wide and narrow, into a temporary steel ring. Looking like upside-down buckets, the barrels are blasted with steam, which makes the staves flexible enough to be bent into a barrel shape and secured with additional steel rings.

Next, the barrels are toasted, in a process much like toasting bread. The interior of a barrel is heated to a specified temperature for a specific time period and emerges darker than the exterior. This process releases substances that will flavor the bourbon and caramelizes sugars that will also color it.

During charring, the insides of the barrels are burned with an open flame; think of overdoing it with a marshmallow on a stick. Cooperages smell like roasted marshmallows, in fact. The resulting charcoal will filter unwanted flavors from the bourbon. The barrelheads, meanwhile, are charred under an open flame in their own oven, and a trench is cut around the edge to fit onto the barrel.

After the barrels are cooled, they're fitted with barrelheads on each end and then they receive their permanent steel hoops. There are three kinds of hoops: two head hoops, which are nearest the ends; two quarter

hoops, just inside the head hoops; and two bilge hoops, nearest the middle, or bilge, of the barrel. Cooperages mark the rivets that hold the hoops together with an identifying letter; for instance, any barrel that has *B* on its rivets was made by the Brown-Forman Cooperage.

Finally, the bunghole, through which the bourbon will be poured into and out of the barrel, is drilled into the middle of a wide stave at a spot equidistant from each head.

No nails or glue are used on barrels; they are held together by the pressure of the staves against each other and against the hoops. A weak spot means expensive leakage at best and complete collapse of a barrel at worst. So before a barrel is released to a distillery, workers pour about a gallon of water into it and rotate it to cover the inside, then apply air pressure to make sure it's airtight. If there are bubbles or leaks, the barrel is sent to the most experienced coopers, who repair it by hand.

Sampling the goods at Jim Beam Distillery (Photo courtesy of Beam Suntory)

Put a Cork in It

When you open a bottle of bourbon, you probably don't think much about the stopper, beyond the satisfying squeak it makes as you remove it. But as you're pouring your next glass, take a closer look at that little piece of cork. It has traveled thousands of miles to keep your bottle sealed—and it may very well be older than the liquid inside it.

Bourbon is aged in barrels made of white oak. Cork comes from another type of oak tree, one called, appropriately enough, the cork oak. But while a white oak tree can yield just one barrel in its lifetime, a cork oak provides the raw material for hundreds of thousands of corks during its 200-year lifespan.

That's because cork can be harvested from a mature cork oak every nine years without harming the tree. The bark is sliced into large sections with a machete and then peeled away from the tree—very much like shearing a sheep for its wool. At peak maturity, around 80 years old, a cork tree can yield up to 440 pounds of cork, enough for 25,000 natural wine corks.

Cork oak trees grow in Spain, southern France, Italy, and North Africa, but more than half of the world's cork comes from Portugal. That's where the family-run Jelinek Cork Group, one of the oldest cork companies in the world, sources the raw material for its products. Founded in 1855 in what is now the Czech Republic, JCG is currently headquartered in Canada and has subsidiaries around the world.

JCG director Sonny Jelinek, the fifth generation in the family business, opened a location in 2013 in Savannah, Georgia, where he makes cork products of all kinds, including bulletin boards, wall tiles, flooring, custom boat decking, even yoga mats.

Jelinek also makes custom stoppers for alcoholic beverages including probably the most distinctive bourbon stopper in the world: the pewter horse and jockey atop every bottle of Blanton's. When the eight different stoppers in the Blanton's series are lined up in order, the positions of the horse's legs represent a full stride, and the tiny letters stamped near one of the hooves spell out *B-L-A-N-T-O-N'-S.*

A worker loosens the bark from a cork oak tree. (Photo courtesy Jelinek Cork Group)

Cork bark after the harvest. (Photo courtesy Jelinek Cork Group)

At a trade show, Jelinek Cork Group displays a sliver of cork oak bark with stoppers punched out of it. (Photo: Carla Carlton)

80

Special-education high school students glue the pewter tops to the cork stoppers and pack them in boxes as part of an apprenticeship program created by Design for Ability, a local nonprofit organization. The students have the opportunity to work for pay during the summer and to be hired on at Jelinek after they graduate.

"This is great for Sonny. He gets to train his people before they are actually put on the payroll, which is to me a win–win situation," says Willie Mobley of Design for Ability. "Even if he doesn't have a position to hire them, they have learned a work ethic and work habits."

The students take great pride in their ability to spy imperfections in the stoppers—the most likely piece to break is the raised arm of the jockey on the S—and to nestle them just so in the egg crate–like trays that are stacked in the boxes.

"I focus hard; I pay attention; I take my time," one student says. "I make them look spotless."

Below: Willie Mobley of Design by Ability, the nonprofit group that provides job opportunities for high school special-education students *(above),* glues Blanton's stoppers together while students package completed ones. (Photos: Harper Carlton)

Sonny Jelinek, the fifth generation of the Jelinek family to make cork products, displays his company's handiwork at a trade show in Louisville, Kentucky. (Photo: Carla Carlton)

Make Mine a Double: The Big Business of Bourbon

"Too much of anything is bad, but too much good whiskey is barely enough."

—*Mark Twain*

AS I WRITE THIS, there are more barrels of bourbon aging in Kentucky—more than 6.6 million—than there are citizens living in the Commonwealth—4.4 million. That shakes out to roughly 1.5 barrels per person.

Colin Blake, creative director at the Distilled Spirits Epicenter in Louisville, puts it another way: if you were to throw a party for the whole world and serve only the bourbon that is now aging in Kentucky, every person on the planet could enjoy about four drinks apiece.

It should be noted that Blake is not advocating that those earthlings under the legal drinking age should indulge; nor am I. We just don't want to redo the math. But bourbon is causing a lot of people to do math these days—mostly addition and multiplication. And many of the numbers have dollar signs in front of them.

For example: distilling is now an $8.5 billion–per–year industry in the state.

Kentucky distillers have increased bourbon production by more than 315% since the turn of the century. In 1999, they made just less than half a million (455,078) barrels of bourbon; in 2015, they made 1,886,821, smashing records back to 1967. "In a little more than a decade, annual bourbon production has more than doubled," says Eric Gregory, president of the Kentucky Distillers'

US BOURBON PRODUCTION: 1967–2015

YEAR	NEW PRODUCTION	TOTAL BOURBON INVENTORY
1967	1,922,009	8,594,588
1968	1,731,446	8,706,688
1969	1,653,901	8,609,815
1970	1,381,309	8,491,893
1971	1,171,858	7,877,969
1972	1,081,542	7,514,642
1973	1,004,877	7,285,998
1974	748,722	6,683,654
1975	685,564	6,148,587
1976	746,646	5,601,334
1977	782,801	5,274,345
1978	666,234	4,952,891
1979	926,234	4,747,614
1980	706,817	4,773,943
1981	851,937	4,815,179
1982	922,847	4,826,545
1983	786,466	4,757,435
1984	793,667	4,704,861
1985	585,369	4,560,105
1986	415,277	4,281,693
1987	289,667	3,906,856
1988	386,556	3,644,959
1989	692,632	3,643,491
1990	790,636	3,668,623
1991	702,930	3,727,483
1992	656,977	3,734,878
1993	567,055	3,678,898
1994	576,416	3,644,680
1995	639,944	3,658,473
1996	529,078	3,531,473
1997	516,795	3,501,667
1998	595,358	3,546,347
1999	455,078	3,437,062
2000	572,260	3,380,403
2001	711,294	3,528,161
2002	718,564	3,614,454
2003	765,031	3,682,479
2004	806,423	3,775,502
2005	906,839	4,059,660
2006	946,326	4,316,812
2007	937,865	4,539,575
2008	794,091	4,600,962
2009	645,503	4,675,220
2010	786,778	4,744,041
2011	988,407	4,922,688
2012	1,007,703	4,982,508
2013	1,116,198	5,294,988
2014	1,306,375	5,669,682
2015	1,886,821	6,657,063

Association (KDA). And with 6,657,063 barrels aging in Kentucky rickhouses in 2015, "we are at the highest inventory now in over 40 years," he says.

{ *Just* A SIP }

The last time Kentucky had more barrels in warehouses than the current 6.6 million was 1974, with nearly 6.7 million. A gallon of gas cost 55 cents, and another product of Kentucky, Muhammad Ali, defeated George Foreman in the "Rumble in the Jungle" to regain his heavyweight title.

(Continued on page 88)

THE DISTILLED SPIRITS EPICENTER

Kentucky isn't just where people come to drink bourbon—it's where they come to learn how to make it.

Since 2012, more than 800 aspiring distillers from 43 states and 7 countries have attended Moonshine University at the Distilled Spirits Epicenter in downtown Louisville. The 4,000-square-foot Epicenter is located next door to Flavorman, a beverage-development lab that has helped hundreds of companies, such as Jones Soda, develop their brands. Both are owned by Dave Dafoe, who once worked for Master Distiller Lincoln Henderson at Brown-Forman in Louisville.

The Epicenter's Grease Monkey Distillery, housed in the bay of a former auto garage, has a complete distilling system made by Louisville's Vendome Copper & Brass Works that includes a 250-gallon cooker, three 250-gallon fermenters, a 250-gallon pot still, and a 20-tray copper vodka column. It's

Grease Monkey Distillery (Photo courtesy of the Kentucky Distillers' Association)

here that Moonshine University students get hands-on experience in producing a batch of bourbon, or any other distilled spirit.

But the real product of the Epicenter is new distillers. Distilling was once a craft handed down from one generation to the next. That still happens at some large commercial distilleries, such as Jim Beam, but Prohibition essentially wiped out the family tradition when home distilling was banned. "It's such a funny history," says John Pogue, distiller at his family's craft distillery, Old Pogue, in Maysville, Kentucky. "It's almost illegal for people to even understand the bourbon-making process since we've outlawed distilling at home."

The Epicenter is a one-stop shop for all distilling needs, operations manager Kevin Hall says. But the most popular offering at its Moonshine University is the 5-Day Distiller Course, an intensive week that covers every aspect of the industry, from selecting grains to marketing a final product. Because the Epicenter belongs to the Kentucky Distillers' Association, the faculty includes Master Distillers from other KDA members, such as Chris Morris of Brown-Forman, Jimmy Russell of Wild Turkey, and Pat Heist of Wilderness Trail Distillery.

Two of the 30 participants in the very first 5-Day Distiller Course in 2013 were Ryan Thompson and Christian Avignon of Vail, Colorado, who said they hoped to open Vail's first distillery. They did just that in September 2014 with 10th Mountain Whiskey & Spirit Company, where they produce two barrels per day.

Other distilleries begun by Moonshine University graduates include Kentucky Peerless Distilling Co. and Copper & Kings American Brandy Company, both in Louisville; Sugarlands Distilling Company in Gatlinburg, Tennessee; Old Forge Distillery in Pigeon Forge, Tennessee; KO Distilling in Manassas, Virginia; and Copper Horse Distilling in Columbia, South Carolina.

In response to the general boom in all things bourbon, the Epicenter added a one-day Bourbon Making Workshop ($500 per person for advanced enthusiasts—a sort of NASCAR Racing Experience of bourbon. Although the course was designed for aficionados who have no intention of opening a distillery, about half of the attendees eventually come back to the Epicenter to attend the 5-Day Distiller Course.

(Continued from page 86)

Bourbon inventory steadily declined from 1974 until 2006, when the numbers started to go back up. During each year from 2012 to 2015, Kentucky distillers' combined total production has exceeded the million-barrel mark. And consumer demand for whiskey just keeps growing.

Overall sales of bourbon, rye, and Tennessee whiskey increased by 5.4% in 2015, thanks to thirsts both foreign and domestic, says an economic-impact study conducted in 2016 by the University of Louisville's Urban Studies Institute in conjunction with the KDA. Kentucky alone exported $311 million of whiskey to other countries in 2015, up $10 million from 2010, according to the study. Its top five international customers were Canada, the United Kingdom, Mexico, China and France, according to US Census Bureau Foreign Trade data.

"Bourbon has started to get a more level playing field with Scotch, its number-one competitor," Gregory says. "People who had never really tasted it before are finding that they like it. For the first time ever, we've seen the international bourbon market overtake the national market in sales."

Sales aren't the only measure of bourbon's importance to Kentucky, however. Bourbon also creates tax revenue—more than $190 million for local and state governments, the economic-impact study says—and good-paying jobs.

So far in the 21st century, the distilling industry has proved to be if not recession-proof, then certainly recession-resilient: while overall manufacturing employment in Kentucky has dropped by 26.3% since 2000, distilling employment has grown by 20.8%, with an average annual salary of $95,089. Kentucky farmers have also benefited from the bourbon boom: use of locally grown corn increased by 65% from 2014 to 2016. Altogether, distilling pours $8.5 billion into Kentucky's economy, an increase of $1 billion in just two years.

{ *Just* A SIP }

There are more than 50 distillers operating in Kentucky now—more than at any time since the repeal of Prohibition.

{ *Just* A SIP }

Kentucky now employs nearly one-third of all the distillery workers in America, and when you factor in the employers who support distilleries— cooperages, grain farmers, equipment manufacturers, trucking companies—more than 17,500 people in Kentucky can thank bourbon for their paychecks. That's 2,000 more than in 2014.

It's almost impossible to believe that in 1991, Buffalo Trace had only 50 employees and was in danger of closing. Today, the Frankfort distillery employs 415 people and has the capacity to produce 1,000 barrels per day. "I used to say, 'When I retire, I hope we're at two shifts,' " says Master Distiller Harlen Wheatley. "We hit that mark two and a half years ago." He expects production capacity to increase again soon.

In July 2015, Buffalo Trace opened a $20 million distribution center that uses satellite technology to store and fetch pallets of all those finished spirits. The three cranes at this automated storage and retrieval system (AS/RS) can move 165 pallets per hour. The project was part of a $71 million investment by parent company Sazerac in its three distilleries in Kentucky. The Glenmore Distillery in Owensboro opened an AS/RS distribution center with four cranes in April 2016, and the Barton 1792 Distillery in Bardstown added equipment to increase its production capacity.

Collectively, Kentucky distilleries have invested more than $400 million since 2008 in capital improvements such as new stills, bottling lines, and warehouses, as well as enhanced visitor centers. Another $630 million in projects is planned over the next five years, including the construction of several brand-new distilleries (see "Pouring Money into Mash," page 98).

The number of licensed distilleries has quintupled since 2011, from 10 to more than 50, as a new crop of microdistilleries, or so-called craft distillers, has emerged nationally in the past five years. There are now two tiers of craft membership: introductory (100 barrels or fewer in inventory) and established (100–10,000 barrels). With these new members, the KDA now represents 33 distilleries—and, like their big brothers, the little guys

89

are growing, too. "The ones that came on in 2011 or 2012 are now on their second or third expansions, and the ones that have just come on are already seeing increase in demand," Gregory says. Dozens more are in the pipeline.

Even so, while Kentucky pretty much owns bourbon production in America, the state ranks just 11th nationwide in total numbers of distilleries, behind places like California, Washington, and Oregon, where craft breweries really took off in the late 1980s. In 1990, there were seven craft distillers in America, says Michael Kinstlick, who is considered a leading expert on the US craft-distilling industry and has presented research to the American Distilling Institute (ADI). By the end of 2016, there were about 1,300.

Somewhat ironically, it was the megadistillers that rose following Prohibition—most of them in Kentucky—that helped spark the craft distillery movement by creating the super-premium bourbon category in the 1990s. The public's embrace of these limited-edition, higher-priced bourbons made it possible for smaller entrepreneurs to succeed with a low volume of innovative specialty spirits. The ADI says that the spirit most commonly being distilled by crafters is whiskey (though not bourbon, necessarily), followed by vodka and gin.

90

The growth of craft distilling in Kentucky, which lies firmly inside the Bible Belt, has been hampered for years by antiquated laws regulating alcohol. It wasn't until 2013, for instance, that the Kentucky General Assembly voted to lift the 1880s-era ban on Election Day alcohol sales during polling hours, a provision originally designed to prevent voter fraud when polling stations were located in saloons.

So perhaps the surest sign that bourbon has become big business in the past several years is the number of laws at both the local and state levels that have changed to accommodate it, even encourage it. Voters in recent local-option elections have approved the sales and/or production of alcohol in precincts, cities, and counties where the consumption of spirits has long been regarded as dangerous at best and sinful at worst. "There are counties going wet that I never thought I'd see in my lifetime," Gregory says.

On March 28, 2016, he giddily witnessed something else he never thought he'd see: the 100-member Kentucky House of Representatives passed a landmark pro-alcohol bill by a vote of 76–20. "I've been in Frankfort [the state capital] for 26 years, and I've never seen a pro-alcohol bill get more than 60 votes. You see that culture changing in Kentucky, because people understand now that bourbon means jobs and tax revenue."

Senate Bill 11 was aimed at helping to increase another growing segment of the bourbon industry: tourism. Distilleries have cleared one big hurdle in recent years as communities voted to allow samples and sales on Sundays. Among other things, SB11 further allows distilleries in wet territories to sell by the drink to visitors (in other words, offer cocktails mixed with their products) and increases the size of free samples from 1 ounce to 1.75 ounces. It also increases the amount of liquor that a distillery can sell to an adult visitor to 9 liters from 3. "The bottle-sales issue was big for us," Gregory says. "People get frustrated when they can only buy three bottles. They want to take them home. You run into Jimmy Russell at Wild Turkey—that's a religious experience. You want his autograph on bottles to take back to friends."

For distilleries in dry territories, the bill allows local-option precinct elections on whether to allow liquor sales in the area that includes the distillery. Senate Bill 11 sends a clear message, Gregory said immediately following its passage: "Kentucky is the one true and authentic home of bourbon."

91

If there's any downside to the current bourbon boom, it's that distillers occasionally run short of product. Remember, they had to predict four to eight years ago, or more, how much bourbon and rye you'd want to drink today, and sometimes they're caught by surprise. When demand outstrips supply, distillers go on "allocations," meaning they limit the number of bottles they ship out until they can catch back up. Liquor stores, bars, and other outlets that sell the most of their products get larger allocations. Distillers might also consider a temporary price increase on the theory that higher prices will slow sales until supply rebounds. But that's a pretty big gamble these days, when there are so many other options out there.

In February 2013, Maker's Mark made its fans see red when the company announced that, due to low supply, it would begin decreasing the alcohol by volume (ABV) of its flagship bourbon by 3%, from 45 to 42, by adding more water. That would lead to a corresponding proof reduction to 84 from 90. The reaction was swift and searing. You just don't mess with a beloved brand (New Coke, anyone?). The company quickly decided to restore Maker's to its original proof and asked fans to bear with them until supply caught up with demand. That made collector's items out of the few 84-proof bottles that ended up on shelves, prompting speculation that the entire thing had been a publicity stunt.

The story behind Wild Turkey Forgiven, also released in 2013, was similarly questioned. A mingling of bourbon and rye, it was said to have resulted from a mistake in the tank room. Once everyone tasted it, though, they loved it—and all was forgiven.

"A lot of people think that was a marketing spiel. I told them I wished it was!" Jimmy Russell explained to me soon after. "We're already short of rye whiskey. We didn't know six or seven years ago that rye was going to do this. We can't turn the faucet on overnight."

Speculation also runs wild when any brand drops the age statement from its label. After bourbon is aged for at least four years, no age statement is required, but many brands list one anyway, since older bourbon is generally considered better bourbon. If you mingle several batches, though, the age statement has to be the age of the youngest barrel. So when an age statement disappears, the fear is that the distiller has begun mingling in younger whiskey to stretch a dwindling supply of older juice.

Bourbon consumers are better educated than ever before, and they are very vocal when something doesn't seem quite right. They want their distillers to be as transparent about their processes as the spirit filling their bottles. A flurry of breathless news stories in 2014, for instance, claimed to blow the lid off a big industry "secret": your "craft" bourbon or rye whiskey was very likely made at MGP, a factory distillery in

Mistake turned masterpiece: Wild Turkey Forgiven (Photo courtesy of Wild Turkey)

Lawrenceburg, Indiana, that has no brand of its own and supplies whiskey in bulk to other companies.

{ *Just* A SIP }

The contents of one barrel can fill anywhere from 150 to 250 bottles. Factors that affect the yield include length and location of aging and whether the whiskey is bottled at barrel strength or gauged down with water.

Many young distilleries do buy bulk whiskey so that they have something to sell until their own bourbon has aged sufficiently. They carefully select barrels and mingle them to achieve the taste profile that their own whiskey will exhibit. The folks behind the Jefferson's Reserve line, on the other hand, have no intention of ever operating a distillery, and their excellent bourbons demonstrate just how tasty mingled products can be. In short, the practice is fairly common and perfectly legal—as long as you don't make false

(Continued on page 95)

 A NOSE FOR BOURBON

Nancy Fraley couldn't have known it at the time, but a chance happening when she was 7 foreshadowed her eventual career: after setting her soda on a table at a wedding reception, she picked up the wrong glass when she returned. "It ended up being some bourbon and Coke," she says. "I thought, 'Wow, that's actually not bad.' "

Nancy Fraley noses a sample in the warehouse. (Photo courtesy of Nosing Services)

Today, Fraley helps craft distillers create or perfect the flavors of their own bourbons, brandies, and rums. She does so by following her nose. Most of what we perceive as "taste" is actually information provided by our sense of smell, and Fraley's olfactory powers are the stuff of legend in the industry. This does not always seem like a gift, she says. "I would have to say, a lot of life is not about pleasant aroma." However, her ability to discern off notes in a particular distillate can mean the difference between a terrific whiskey and a terrible one.

"You have to start with a quality distillate," she says. Barrels add flavor and color, but they can do only so much. "Aging should enhance the spirit, not work as a masking tool."

Fraley earned a law degree and worked in a law firm for a short time, until she tasted a revelatory brandy at a fundraiser in 2006 that had been made by Hubert Germain-Robin in Ukiah, California. She quit her job; did some traveling in the Armagnac brandy-producing region of France; and studied distillation, fermentation, and maturation. A year later she was working at Germain-Robin. (She was so taken by the spirit that her dog's name is Brandy.)

Today, her Nosing Services company handles anywhere from 10 to 25 distillery clients at a time, all over the world. When I spoke with her in December 2015, she had just returned to her California home from Haiti, where she had helped a client put barrels of *rhum agricole,* or cane juice rum, in the client's warehouse, and she was heading to Australia in January. Her schedule was already booked through September.

While Fraley is still called on to fix problems, she says new craft distillers are a lot savvier than they were even two years ago. "Most have done their research. They've gone out and learned something about the whole distilling world and everything that entails. And they realize that if they aren't talented enough to make the product themselves, they can hire someone else to do it."

Many craft distillers ask her to develop their spirits' particular aroma and taste profile. After she formulates the mash bill, she makes sure they have the right warehousing conditions, and then she matches the distillate with the proper barrels. "Whenever possible, I like to direct them to high-quality cooperage. If you think about the life of a distillate, I like to say it's conceived during fermentation, gestates in a copper womb, and matures in the barrel. The French refer to it as *elevage*—the art of barrel maturation, essentially. Literally it means to raise your barrels the way you would your own children."

Six months to a year after the whiskey is in the barrels, she returns to take notes on how the juice is maturing. That first time, she says, "I taste every barrel." In one case, that meant pushing through 200 a day to get through a client's 6,000-barrel inventory. "I don't recommend this, for me or anyone else! It's intense. But I have to know someone's stock." Some barrels may need to be moved, either to speed up or to slow down the maturation process. So-called "honey barrels" are noted, too. "We will want to nurture that area—those could be single-barrel rock stars."

But most barrels will end up being part of a blend, and this is where Fraley really shines. She uses what's known as a pyramid structure. The bottom layer is the base profile of the whiskey. The contents of these barrels are nice, but unremarkable. "Maybe they are a little dry. Maybe I'm not getting enough mouthfeel. Maybe I want more sweetness." In the middle tier, she will select whiskey from barrels that fills those gaps. "The top would be what I refer to as the nuance components—something really spicy or fruity or floral that will make that blend pop, give it a little more passion or interest."

While distilling and fermentation are all about science, Fraley says, blending is an art. "I've devised ways to think about it, but it's a little like oil painting: you can teach technique, but you can't just create a Matisse."

95

(Continued from page 93)

claims on your bottle about the origin of the spirit inside. Whiskey drinkers are pretty mellow people, but they don't like to be tricked.

Iowa-based Templeton Rye found this out the hard way. In July 2015, the distiller settled three class action lawsuits that accused Templeton of intentionally misleading consumers by labeling its whiskey as a small-batch rye made in Iowa when it actually sourced the juice from MGP. The settlement agreement required Templeton to change its labels and website and set up a $2.5 million fund to refund customers who had bought bottles of the whiskey.

Of course, some lawsuits are just silly. A federal judge in Florida dismissed a class action against Maker's Mark in 2015 that took issue with the company labeling its bourbon as "handmade" when, in fact, machinery is used during the production process. Taken literally, the court wrote, all bourbon is handmade, because it does not spontaneously occur in nature; taken less literally, "no reasonable consumer could believe" that bourbon could be made without commercial-scale equipment: "In sum, no reasonable person would understand 'handmade' in this context to mean literally made by hand." (In other breaking news, Keebler cookies are not really made by elves who live in a tree.)

There is, however, no official definition for *craft distillery*. To organizations like the KDA and the ADI, the term simply means distilleries of a certain size, with a fairly small output. But to the public, says Joe Heron, owner of Copper & Kings American Brandy Company in Louisville, it can imply authenticity and artisan craftsmanship. "To consumers, and particularly millennial consumers, it's a badge of individualism and quality," he says, as in craft beer versus Budweiser.

"But craft beer had an easy target," he adds. "Mass-produced beer is pretty bland. I don't believe that's true of the spirits business."

Nor does Jim Rutledge, former Master Distiller at Four Roses. "There is more of an art here, I think. We've learned through the years what it takes to make a good bourbon. We've had our ups and downs and trial and error. And it's not something that you fool around with and you have to wait five or six years to find out if what you did today turned out good. And it's not something you can learn overnight."

Distiller Charlie Downs has a unique perspective on the subject. At Heaven Hill's main distilling plant, where he worked for most of his career, he oversaw production of 935 barrels per day. As the Artisanal Distiller at Heaven Hill's new Evan Williams Bourbon Experience, a microdistillery in downtown Louisville, his daily output is slightly less: one barrel.

Machines at Heaven Hill's main plant ensure that the production line runs at a consistent pace, opening and closing valves and adjusting steam pressure. At the Bourbon Experience, Downs does all of that by hand. But even in the larger setting, it is people, not machines, who set taste profiles and maintain the quality of the bourbon—and have for the entirety of Heaven Hill's 80-year history.

"Whether we're mass-producing 1,000 barrels a day or 1, we are still taking pride in what we are doing," Downs says. "We know that we have to produce a superior product to carry on the tradition and the legacy of what has come from the Master Distillers before us. It's a great privilege to do that."

Top: Tasting bar at Copper & Kings American Brandy Distillery; *bottom:* artisanal still at the Evan Williams Bourbon Experience (Photos: top, Carla Carlton; bottom, courtesy of Heaven Hill)

Pouring Money into Mash

Since 2008, every major distillery in Kentucky has responded to the growing thirst for bourbon by taking steps to increase production, improve visitor experiences, or both—capital improvements that together equal more than $400 million in investment. In 2016, meanwhile, half a dozen large new distilleries, and at least that many craft distilleries, were under construction.

FOUR ROSES In June 2015, Four Roses Bourbon announced a $54 million expansion that would double production. The improvements include two buildings and new equipment at its distillery in Lawrenceburg and four new warehouses at its warehouse and bottling facility in Cox's Creek. Since 2012, Four Roses has expanded the visitor center in Lawrenceburg and created a visitor center in Cox's Creek, allowing the bottling facility to join the Kentucky Bourbon Trail tour (see page 124).

HEAVEN HILL This family-owned and -operated spirits producer celebrated its 80th anniversary in 2015 by announcing a third expansion at its main plant, Bernheim Distillery in Louisville. In 1935, when the first barrel was filled, Heaven Hill had the capacity to mash 500 bushels of corn a day; today it mashes 12,150 bushels a day.

JIM BEAM Jim Beam is the top-selling premium bourbon in the world, but until 2012, it had one of the most bottom-shelf distillery visitor experiences in the state. That year, Beam opened the **Jim Beam American Stillhouse,** a beautiful and interactive center from which it launched the first-ever tours of the distillery. That same year, a new **Global Innovation Center** on the distillery grounds began work on research and development of new products. In October 2015, Beam opened the **Jim Beam Urban Stillhouse,** an interactive tourist attraction in downtown Louisville where visitors can select, label, bottle, and cork their own bottle of bourbon—sort of a Build-A-Bear experience for adults.

MAKER'S MARK In November 2015, this picturesque distillery in Loretto fired up a third still, increasing its production capacity by 50%. Rather

Single-story rickhouses at
Four Roses (Photo: Carla Carlton)

99

(Photo courtesy of Beam Suntory)

The Cellar at Maker's Mark
(Photo: Carla Carlton)

than build a larger still, the company commissioned an exact copy of its first two, choosing to remain, as it puts it, "purposefully inefficient." The still was part of a $70 million investment that also included 2 new boilers, 21 more fermenters, a new grain roller, and up to 25 new warehouses currently under construction. In December 2016, Maker's unveiled "The Cellar." Carved from a limestone shelf and with a 2,000-barrel capacity, it allows Maker's 46 and Private Select to be barrel-finished year round by maintaining a temperature of no more than 50 degrees.

(In 2014, Suntory Holdings of Japan acquired Beam Inc., owner of both Jim Beam and Maker's Mark, to form Beam Suntory, the world's third-largest spirits company. Four Roses is owned by another Japanese company, Kirin, and Wild Turkey is owned by Gruppo Campari of Italy. This foreign ownership makes some people nervous, but so far these companies have done nothing but pour money into the distilleries. "They wouldn't be investing all that money if they was thinkin' about doing away with it," says Wild Turkey's Jimmy Russell. They can't tinker too much with the recipes either, thanks to all the regulations that govern bourbon production. And because bourbon is, by law, a distinct product of the United States, they can't move production to another country.)

MICHTER'S In the 1990s, Joseph J. Magliocco and the late Dick Newman resurrected the historic but abandoned Michter's brand, which had originated in Pennsylvania. In 2011, they announced they would build a distillery in Kentucky to produce the brand. Today, Michter's has two locations in Kentucky: a 67,000-square-foot distillery and bottling facility in the Louisville suburb of Shively, and the iconic Fort Nelson Building on Louisville's Whiskey Row, which the company is restoring as a boutique distillery and tourism destination.

WILD TURKEY Since 2009, when Gruppo Campari acquired Wild Turkey from Pernod Ricard of France, $100 million in improvements have included a new distillery that more than doubled production; a new packaging facility that allows the distillery to once again bottle Wild Turkey on site, as well as all of Gruppo Campari's distilled US brands; and an architecturally stunning, 9,000-square-foot visitor center overlooking the Kentucky River.

101

Wild Turkey Visitor Center (Photo courtesy of Wild Turkey)

WOODFORD RESERVE Brown-Forman has spent more than $35 million at its distillery in Versailles since 2013, adding new bourbon-maturation warehouses and stills and improving the bottling line. A renovation and expansion of the visitor center added a dedicated tasting room and enlarged the retail space.

New Projects

In a two-week span between mid-April and early May 2016, **Luxco,** a distilled-spirits company in St. Louis, broke ground for one new distillery in Bardstown, and the new **Bardstown Bourbon Company** installed a 50-foot-tall still in a second one. Luxco's $30 million Lux Row distillery will have a visitor center and up to six barrel warehouses. The target for opening is late 2017. Luxco also owns a 50% share of **Limestone Branch,** a craft distillery in Lebanon, Kentucky. At the Bardstown Bourbon Company, where a 50-foot still went up on April 14, Steve Nally, former Master Distiller for Maker's Mark, will oversee production of the distillery's own brands, as well as those of partners in its Collaborative Distilling Program.

Still installation at Bardstown Bourbon Company (Photo courtesy of Bardstown Bourbon Company)

Alltech, which operates Town Branch Distillery in Lexington, plans to open the $13 million **Dueling Barrels Brewing & Distilling Co.** in Pikeville in 2017. The first distillery in eastern Kentucky in modern times, it will feature references to the battling Hatfields and McCoys, as well as the region's musical heritage. In November 2016, the makers of **Angel's Envy**, a small-batch bourbon finished in port wine casks that was recently purchased by Bacardi, opened a 100,000-square-foot distillery and visitor center in Louisville in a historic structure directly across Main Street from Louisville Slugger Field.

Angel's Envy Distillery
(Photo courtesy of
Louisville Distilling Co.)

Just a few blocks away, **Brown-Forman** broke ground in July 2015 on its **Old Forester Distillery,** which will double production of the flagship brand introduced by company founder George Garvin Brown in 1870. The $45 million project will also serve as a home place for the Old Forester brand, with tours, a tasting room, exhibits, bourbon-making demonstrations, and event spaces.

103

Architectural rendering
of Old Forester Distillery
(Courtesy of Brown-Forman)

Stitzel-Weller warehouse at the
Bulleit Frontier Bourbon Experience
(Photos courtesy of Diageo)

In October 2014, London-based **Diageo** began work in Shelby County, about 35 miles from downtown Louisville, on a $115 million project that will include a distillery and six barrel warehouses. The **Bulleit Distillery** will produce Bulleit Bourbon, Bulleit Rye, and other Diageo whiskey brands. Bulleit, founded by Tom Bulleit more than 20 years ago, is one of the fastest-growing small batch whiskeys in the United States. Until the distillery opens, fans can continue to visit the **Bulleit Frontier Bourbon Experience** at the Stitzel-Weller Distillery in Shively. The experience, which includes a visitor center, a bottling line, and a small craft still, opened in September 2014.

Like Sleeping Beauty—or, perhaps more accurately, her thorn-covered castle—a historic distillery in Woodford County has been awakened from decades of slumber and neglect. The **Old Taylor Distillery** was the most beautiful of the seven Kentucky distilleries that Col. Edmund Haynes "E. H." Taylor Jr. had a hand in (one of them, the present-day Buffalo

Trace, honors him with its Col. E.H.   105
Taylor line of whiskeys). Built to resemble
a castle with turrets and located on vast
landscaped grounds that included pergolas,
pools, and an elaborate springhouse with Roman columns, Old Taylor sat
empty and abandoned after closing in 1972. In 2014, investors Will Arvin
and Wes Murry purchased the distillery and began a $6 million restora-
tion. They announced in February 2016 that it would be renamed **Castle
& Key.** Most notably, they hired Marianne Barnes, the first female Master Distiller in modern times, to produce their spirits. Barnes, a chemical engineer, had risen to the position of master taster at Brown-Forman
before she made the move to Castle & Key. The distillery is expected to
open to the public in 2017.

Finally, in May 2016, bourbon fans were surprised to learn that Jim
Rutledge, the longtime Master Distiller at Four Roses who retired in September 2015, plans a distillery of his own near Louisville. **J. W. Rutledge
Distillery** plans to distill Kentucky bourbon and rye, as well as a wheated
bourbon, using two or more yeast strains and several mash bills.

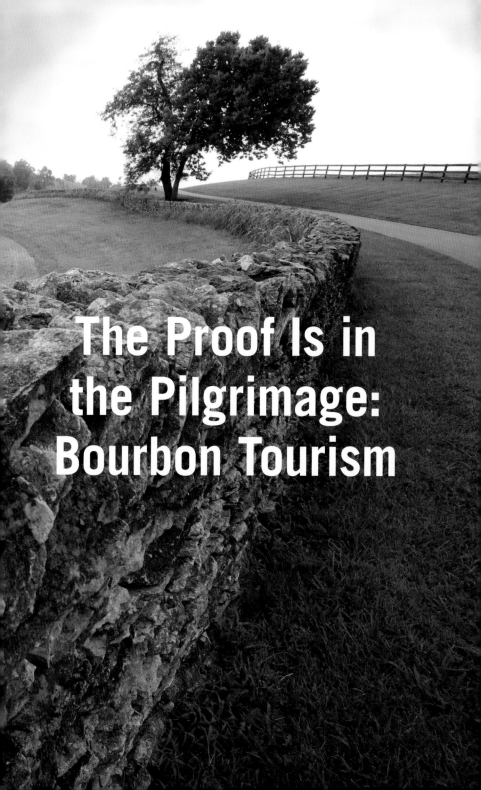

The Proof Is in
the Pilgrimage:
Bourbon Tourism

"I'd much rather be someone's shot of whiskey
than everyone's cup of tea."

—*Carrie Bradshaw (Sarah Jessica Parker)*, Sex and the City

TEN YEARS AGO, a visit to the Wild Turkey distillery in Lawrenceburg, Kentucky, could be something of a letdown. The visitor center
was a 1,000-square-foot house built in the 1800s that had been converted
for that purpose, if by "converted" you mean opening it up into one room
and stocking it with T-shirts and shot glasses. You didn't have to call
ahead for a tour, because at most there'd be only 10 or so other people
milling around waiting for one. You'd all head on up to the distillery
in a van and take a look around, then return to the little house for
a tasting—unless you'd made the mistake of arriving on a Sunday,
when local liquor laws prohibited the distillery from offering you a sip
or selling you a bottle.

Visit the Wild Turkey Visitor Center today, however, and you might
think you've accidentally stepped into a cathedral. Rising on a bluff that
overlooks the Kentucky River, the 9,000-square-foot stained-wood structure has a simple silhouette meant to evoke the tobacco barns that were
once common in central Kentucky. But no tobacco barn ever had a wall
made entirely of glass. When the sun shines bright, the amber glow off the

109

The architecture of the Wild Turkey Visitor Center artfully evokes a classic Kentucky tobacco barn. (Photo courtesy of Wild Turkey)

wood that encloses a ramped promenade is as warm as the bourbon in the glasses that await you in the elevated tasting room—even on Sunday.

Opened in 2014 at a cost of $4 million, the Visitor Center was designed to accommodate the approximately 80,000 guests per year who now visit "The House That Jimmy Built," as a billboard in front of the distillery declares it. Milestones in the life of legendary Master Distiller Jimmy Russell, who celebrated his 60th anniversary with Wild Turkey the same year the Visitor Center opened, are captured on a timeline along one wall. The newer, larger gift shop offers limited-edition bottles, some available only at the distillery and all available for purchase every day of the week, thanks to a local-option election in 2007.

Like Wild Turkey, most established Kentucky distilleries have expanded in recent years to contain the number of bourbon enthusiasts pouring into the state.

The Kentucky Distillers' Association tapped into an international thirst when it established the Kentucky Bourbon Trail in 1999 and then the Kentucky Bourbon Trail Craft Tour in 2012. The trails are an avenue for distillers "to promote authenticity and craftsmanship to their customers, and make them ambassadors," says KDA president Eric Gregory. Distilleries not on the official trail, such as Buffalo Trace and Barton 1792, are also seeing record numbers of visitors.

{ *Just* A SIP }

In 2016, visits along the Kentucky Bourbon Trail and Craft Tour topped 1 million—a new attendance record. The attraction has grown 300% since its 1999 founding.

Providing an engaging personal experience to a bourbon enthusiast is more valuable than any advertising, says Wild Turkey's Jimmy Russell. "You can do all the advertisement you want to in magazines and everything like that. I might read it, but how many people do I tell about it? But if you come on a tour like the Kentucky Bourbon Trail, you get back home and they ask you, 'What did you do?' 'Well, I went to this bourbon distillery and that bourbon distillery. They showed us this. They showed us that.' I've had a lot of people come here [who have said], 'Well, the reason we're here is that our friends was here last year and enjoyed being on the Bourbon Trail.' "

Sure, there are places other than Kentucky where you can tour a bourbon distillery—more and more all the time, in fact, as the craft-distilling movement continues to grow. But only in Kentucky will you find 200 years of bourbon-making history. Bourbon flows through the narrative of the Bluegrass just as limestone-filtered springs flow through its gently rolling hills. If you want to know the complete story of bourbon, you must come to the Commonwealth. "Kentucky is the birthplace, the home place, of bourbon, the point of origin," says Chris Morris, Master Distiller at Brown-Forman.

And like the winery trails of the Napa and Sonoma Valleys in California, Kentucky's Bourbon Trail combines immersive distillery experiences with singular scenic drives.

"People go to Kentucky for bourbon, but part of it is that it's a fantastic place—such a beautiful drive any time of the year," says Paul Tomaszewski, a Louisiana native and co-owner with his wife, Merry Beth Roland Tomaszewski, of MB Roland Distillery in Pembroke, which lies along the Tennessee border in the western part of the state. "You don't have many places like Kentucky."

The dramatic seasonal fluctuations that make Kentucky particularly well suited for bourbon maturation also provide an ever-changing visual feast: the bright green leaves of spring punctuated by the vivid dark pink of redbuds and the white lace petticoats of dogwoods; the summer fields of corn, tassels waving to the blue chicory blooms bobbing alongside the road; the blazing orange and red autumn finery of sweet maples; and the smudged blues and browns of winter, rolling hills sometimes dusted with, and occasionally buried in, snow.

111

{ *Just* A SIP }

"Heaven must be a Kentucky kind of place," Daniel Boone has been quoted as saying. He probably never really uttered those words, but as he's been dead for almost 200 years, we can't exactly ask him. Also, guess where he and Mrs. Boone are buried? That's right: Kentucky. Frankfort, to be exact.

While there are several distilleries clustered near larger Kentucky cities such as Louisville, Lexington, and Frankfort, you might have to drive as much as an hour or more between craft distillers. But you'll savor the trip along with the sipping. You're likely to see sleek Thoroughbreds racing across a pasture corralled by white or black plank fences, with a horse barn in the distance that is larger and much grander than the adjacent farmhouse. You might still catch some golden-brown tobacco leaves hanging to dry.

You'll cross rivers, streams, and lakes, and drive through cuts where a hillside was blasted to make way for the road, revealing layers upon layers of limestone. Especially in central Kentucky, you'll notice that many roads are lined by stone fences; these were hand-stacked (no mortar!) by Irish immigrants in the 19th century for landowners who wanted to mimic the look of English estates.

{ *Just* A SIP }

The Irish particularly loved Kentucky because its verdant green hills reminded them of home. Their fences are so cherished that during a 2003 project to widen Paris Pike, a 12.5-mile stretch of road between Lexington and Paris, Kentucky, the state shelled out extra money to move and rebuild the stone fences along the route.

And you'll pass through charming places such as Bardstown, the self-proclaimed "Bourbon Capital of the World," which Rand McNally/*USA Today* once christened "the most beautiful small town in America." Bardstown is the site of the annual Kentucky Bourbon Festival in September. If you visit then, you're as likely to have to wait for a limousine full of bourbon tourists making a left turn as you are to pass a tractor on the highway leading into town.

When you arrive at your destination, you will enjoy an experience that feeds all of the senses. If the distillery is making bourbon, you'll smell the mash before you're even inside—a heavy, yeasty aroma like the world's best bakery. You'll feel the heat rising off the fermenter as bubbles break on the surface, and perhaps dip your finger into the mash for a tangy taste. You'll hear the clink of bottles being filled on the bottling line. In the dim, dusty

Nestled amid horse farms in Central Kentucky, the
grounds of the Woodford Reserve Distillery in Versailles
are among the Kentucky Bourbon Trail's most scenic.
(Photo courtesy of Brown-Forman)

warehouse, you'll be enveloped by the angels' share, the alcohol that is evaporating from the barrels. Your eyes might sting, but your mouth will definitely water. That thirst will be slaked with a tasting of the distillery's brands at the end of your tour.

You'll realize that even though some aspects are now monitored by computer, making bourbon is still very much a hands-on process of an all-natural agricultural product and, in many cases, a family affair. Your tour guide may be a member of the family that owns the distillery, or someone who might as well be, having worked there for decades. If you're lucky, the Master Distiller might be in the gift shop to sign your bottle.

The year 2016 marked the 10th anniversary of the Kentucky Bourbon Trail passport program (see page 124), in which visitors who have their passports stamped at each of the distilleries on the trail (Angel's Envy in Louisville will join in 2017) receive a complimentary T-shirt. ("You'd think those T-shirts was worth a hundred thousand dollars," says Wild Turkey's Jimmy Russell.) A companion adventure, the Kentucky Bourbon Trail Craft Tour, has stops around the state. Because this sprawling tour takes more time and dedication than the main Bourbon Trail, the reward is a little sweeter: a silver julep cup.

{ *Just* A SIP }

In the Kentucky Bourbon Trail passport program's first year, 186 people completed a passport. By 2015, that number had jumped to 14,226. All told, around 90,000 people have traveled the entire trail. The Kentucky Bourbon Trail Craft Tour, meanwhile, saw a 32% increase in visits to its 11 participating microdistilleries in 2016 (there are now 13 stops).

"It is incredible how many people the trails are bringing into the state," says John Pogue, a distiller at The Old Pogue Distillery in Maysville, a Craft Tour stop along Kentucky's northeastern border with Ohio. Kentucky's 200-year heritage of producing bourbon is a powerful draw, he says. "People want to go where it started." There are those who say that Maysville, once the county seat of Bourbon County, is where it started. Another contingent says otherwise. "It comes up almost every tour," Pogue says. "I don't know if we'll ever be able to answer it. But people are very interested in the history of bourbon."

There is plenty of history to be discovered. On the campus of Buffalo Trace Distillery in Frankfort, Kentucky, for example, sits the recently restored Old Taylor House. Built by Commodore Richard Taylor in 1792, the same year that Kentucky became a state, it is the oldest residential dwelling in Franklin County. Distilling is said to have begun on the site in 1775. The first distillery building was constructed in 1812 by Harrison Blanton. In 1870, Commodore Taylor's great-grandson, Col. Edmund Haynes Taylor Jr., purchased it and named it the Old Fire Copper (OFC) Distillery. Now called Buffalo Trace, the distillery was designated a National Historic Landmark in 2013.

Buffalo Trace Master Distiller Harlen Wheatley recalls once visiting Charleston, South Carolina, and taking a boat tour to Fort Sumter, where the first shots of the Civil War were fired in 1861. "I was thinking, 'Well, we've been making bourbon longer than that,' " he said. "You have to go back another 50 years."

In the eight years that Amy Preske has worked as Buffalo Trace's public relations and events manager, the number of visitors has increased from 50,000 per year to 170,587 in 2016. Wheatley, who has worked there for 20 years, adds, "I remember when we started tours, and the number of visitors was 'zero.'"

Since then, more than 1 million people have made their way to the distillery, which is owned by Sazerac Company, and the visitor center has been expanded three times to hold them all. "We started out with what we thought was a gift shop and a visitor center that would last for 100 years. That lasted two. We then moved into another one and thought, 'Well, this one will last for 1,000 years.' It managed to make it six years," Sazerac CEO Mark Brown said on July 2, 2015, as he cut the ribbon to open a new tasting room and event space on that visitor center's second floor.

Similarly, Brown-Forman Master Distiller Chris Morris remembers walking down from the visitor center of the new Woodford Reserve Distillery in 1996 and wondering, "Will anyone really come here?" The distillery visitor experience opened the same year that Brown-Forman released its boutique brand and is on a distilling site in Versailles, Kentucky, that dates to 1780. The building itself went up in 1838, established by Elijah Pepper and passed on to his son, Oscar Pepper. It was later known as

Labrot & Graham before being purchased by Brown-Forman. Woodford Reserve was designated a National Historic Landmark in 2000.

And people did indeed come, following a curving two-lane road beside a horse farm to arrive at a picture-perfect setting where gray stone buildings hug the Grassy Springs Branch of Glenn's Creek. So many came, in fact—120,000-plus per year at latest count—that in 2014, Brown-Forman invested more than $1.9 million to expand and renovate the Woodford Reserve visitor center, creating a dedicated tasting room, new displays, and a larger gift shop.

Maker's Mark, also a National Historic Landmark, has upgraded its visitor experience twice in recent years, first replacing the small tasting bar in the gift shop with three classroom-style tasting rooms in a working warehouse, where they are separated by glass walls and surrounded by 1,000 barrels of aging bourbon. The rooms doubled the time that can be spent on tasting at the end of a tour, to about 10 minutes from 4 or 5. As part of a $70 million expansion project that began in 2014, Maker's added a new welcome center that encompasses a Victorian house as well as new parking lots and better access roads.

More than 125,000 people made their way in 2015 to the tidy Maker's Mark campus, which is distinguished by dark brown buildings with red

Four Roses' Mission-style buildings
(Photo courtesy of Four Roses)

shutters that each have a cutout shaped like the distinctive Maker's bottle. The number of visitors is even more impressive when you consider that you really have to want to get to Loretto, Kentucky—population 721 on a good day and on the way to exactly nowhere.

Two founding members of the Kentucky Bourbon Trail, Four Roses and Heaven Hill, have each added a second stop in the past four years.

The Four Roses Distillery, which, like Wild Turkey, is located in Lawrenceburg, has the most unusual appearance of any distillery in Kentucky, with its yellow Mission-style architecture. But its one-story warehouses are located in Bullitt County, only several miles away from Jim Beam. For years, this Cox's Creek location was not open to the public. But in 2014, Four Roses opened a 2,500-square-foot visitor center there that features memorabilia from the Four Roses archives. Tours of the warehousing, barreling, and bottling operations are followed by samples at a handsome tasting bar.

Heaven Hill's Bourbon Heritage Center, just outside Bardstown, has as its centerpiece a tasting room that's shaped like a barrel. It's a popular stop on the Bourbon Trail, but even more pilgrims—92,000 in 2015—are now making their way to the family-owned distillery's Evan Williams Bourbon Experience, which opened in 2013 on Main Street in Louisville. Located

Evan Williams Bourbon Experience
(Photo courtesy of Heaven Hill)

just across the street from where Evan Williams, Kentucky's first commercial distiller, built his distillery in 1783, the Experience has a facade dominated by a dramatic five-story Evan Williams bottle that becomes three-dimensional in the two lower floors and pours into a "bourbon fountain" glass in the lobby. The boutique distillery, which produces just one barrel per day, offers an interactive tour and two bars where guests may sample premium Heaven Hill brands.

Because the bourbon is warehoused in Bardstown, "the only thing we haven't been able to re-create is the smell" of the angels' share, says Artisanal Distiller Charlie Downs.

Although Jim Beam is one of the best-selling bourbon brands in the world, for years the distillery had a visitor experience that Master Distiller Fred Noe charitably referred to as "minimal"—a video, a look around the Beam home place, and a gift shop. That changed dramatically in October 2012, when the Jim Beam American Stillhouse opened in Clermont. In a replica of a 1930s-era still house, clad in corrugated metal panels to match the warehouses on the property, visitors take a tour that leads them through the entire bourbon-making process. One highlight is the "stillevator," an elevator that lifts guests to the second floor of the visitor center just as alcohol rises in the still during distillation.

Jim Beam Urban Stillhouse in downtown Louisville (Photo courtesy of Beam Suntory)

Beam Suntory, which owns Jim Beam and Maker's Mark, followed the Stillhouse in 2015 with the Jim Beam Urban Stillhouse in downtown Louisville. In addition to a small working still and a tasting bar, this city cousin includes a sort of "Willy Wonka Bourbon Factory" experience for adults. You label an empty bottle, fill it with Jim Beam Urban Stillhouse Select, cork it, and then place it in a basket that travels overhead and gets its tax stamp before being deposited at the checkout counter.

Louisville's Whiskey Row, a 10-block stretch of Main Street along the Ohio River, was the center of the bourbon universe in the early 1900s, and even now, the city produces one-third of all the bourbon whiskey in the world. But following Prohibition, the distilleries moved out of downtown and the city began to downplay its bourbon heritage. Distilleries didn't open their doors to the public, much less invite them in for tours. It was almost as if, Stacey Yates says in a dramatic stage whisper, "we don't speak of it."

Yates, vice president of marketing communications for the Louisville Convention & Visitors Bureau, began the city's effort to reclaim its place in bourbon history by declaring Louisville "the Gateway to the Kentucky Bourbon Trail" and, in 2008, creating the Urban Bourbon Trail, a curated list of bars and restaurants that promote and celebrate bourbon by offering at least 50 brands and using bourbon in cocktails and some dishes. Highlighting the culinary aspect recognized that bourbon isn't just a drink in Kentucky, she said, "it's a part of the culture and the heritage." The Urban Bourbon Trail has grown from 8 initial stops to almost 40. And just like the Kentucky Bourbon Trail, this trail has a passport program and a T-shirt.

119

For most of the 20th century, the very term "Whiskey Row" had fallen out of the local vernacular. Then one night, Yates was hosting a travel writer for dinner and asked local historian Mike Veach to join them. "We were really trying to seed the 'Bourbon Country' brand. And Mike said something about 'the distillers on Whiskey Row,' and we went, 'What? Where was it? Well, we are going to bring that back.' We started talking about it, and the next thing you know, some entrepreneur had built the Whiskey Row Lofts. That really helped. Now, almost anybody in Louisville you talk to, if you asked them, 'Where's Whiskey Row?' They'd say, 'Oh, that's down on Main Street.'"

120

"Quality people willing to pay quality prices for quality product"
– GEORGE GARVIN BROWN

GGB HOUSE

INTEGRITY CUP

– GEORGE GARVIN BROWN

Rendering of the
Old Forester Distillery
Visitor Center (Photo courtesy
of Brown-Forman)

Angel's Envy, a small-batch bourbon finished in port wine casks that was recently purchased by Bacardi, opened a 100,000-square-foot distillery in November 2016 on Louisville's Main Street in a renovated historic structure across the street from Louisville Slugger Field. Two other distilleries with planned visitor experiences will soon join it along Whiskey Row: Brown-Forman is building an Old Forester Distillery in two historic buildings at 117 and 119 W. Main St. that will allow it to double production of its flagship brand; and Michter's is working to stabilize the Old Fort Nelson Building for a boutique distillery and tour. (See page 102 for more information on these projects; also see page 3 for a map of the area.)

"What is going on with Louisville's Whiskey Row is phenomenal," KDA president Eric Gregory says. "Pretty soon you won't be able to walk from one block to the next without seeing a distillery."

That may be a slight exaggeration. But Mayor Greg Fischer, who was elected in 2010 and is in his second term, embraced bourbon as the "buzz factor" that could help distinguish Louisville from other cities and could be capitalized upon not only to draw tourists but to serve as a point of intrigue to businesses seeking to relocate. His enthusiasm led to the coining of the term "bourbonism."

121

"When I was running for office, it seemed to me that our local food movement was vastly undermarketed and -promoted. And bourbon is a big part of that. Bourbon has tremendous international appeal. It is tremendously authentic. And it is ours. What people want when they visit is a place with soul. It seemed like a no-brainer. This is ours, this is great, we should be promoting it more. Louisvillians in general tend to be understated about these things. If this was in another city, they would have been shouting from the highest mountain, declaring victory already."

Call it what you like, bourbon tourism is a rapidly growing segment of Kentucky's economy. Bourbon tourists, on average, spend $1,000 on a trip and stay longer than typical tourists, according to an economic impact study conducted by the University of Louisville. More than 85% of them come from outside Kentucky.

"Those people are staying in hotels here; they're eating here," says Patrick Heist, distiller at Wilderness Trail Distillery in Danville, where he

Pat Heist conducts a tasting at the Wilderness
Trail Distillery. (Photo: Carla Carlton)

estimates that 95% of his visitors are from out of state—some of them from far out of state. "We had a visit last week from a fairly large group from a Japanese distillery. We've had Australian visitors. We get a lot of bikers from up in Canada who come down and bike the Bourbon Trail."

{ *Just* A SIP }

It's not unusual to encounter one or two international visitors on a tour of any given distillery on any given day. They may not be fluent in Kentuckian—I once had to advise three French surgeons I met at Barton 1792 that their next destination, Woodford Reserve, was located in "Ver-SAYLES," not "Ver-SIGH"—but they are definitely fluent in bourbon.

Master Distiller Fred Noe likes to tell about a woman who came to tour Jim Beam from Australia, where his brand is the top-selling alcoholic spirit of any kind. She said she was "in the neighborhood" to attend a wedding in the United States and figured she'd work in a stop at the distillery. "Where was the wedding?" he asked her. Her response: "California."

The surge of visits to Kentucky bourbon distilleries, which topped 1 million in 2016, has prompted the KDA to undertake a five-year strategic planning process to draw a blueprint for growth, Eric Gregory says. "We've got to make sure we don't do what happened in California, where it just exploded overnight, and then people started having a negative experience. We want to make sure that visitors have that intimate experience. We don't want, you know, 100 to a tour and you can't hear the tour guide and you go back and tell people, 'I went on the Kentucky Bourbon Trail, but it just wasn't that good.' "

The KDA also encourages bourbon tourists to enjoy themselves responsibly. "Bourbon tourism in Kentucky is no longer something you can do in a long weekend—it requires multiple trips," Gregory says. "It's more of an adventure, or a quest. We want people to slow down and savor the trip, like you do in wine country. Make it the elegant vacation that it is, and not a bachelor party rushing from one distillery to another."

123

The Kentucky Bourbon Trail

Collect stamps at all the stops on the Kentucky Bourbon Trail tour in your official passport, and receive a commemorative T-shirt. For days and hours of operation, tour times, and costs, visit kybourbontrail.com. Note that some distilleries shut down production during the summer or drought conditions, so call ahead to be sure they'll be open when you tour.

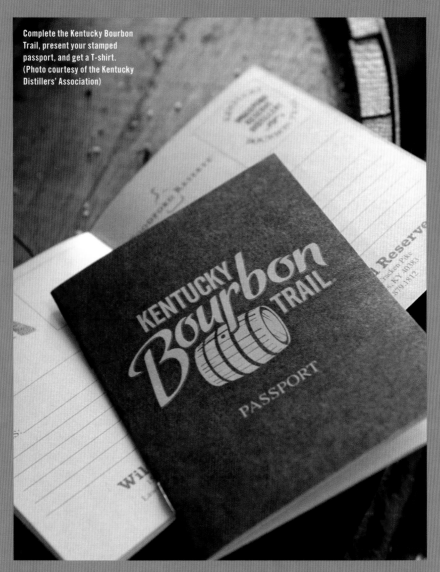

Complete the Kentucky Bourbon Trail, present your stamped passport, and get a T-shirt. (Photo courtesy of the Kentucky Distillers' Association)

Bulleit Bourbon Frontier Whiskey (Photo courtesy of Diageo)

BULLEIT FRONTIER WHISKEY EXPERIENCE

3860 Fitzgerald Road, Louisville, KY 40216

bulleitexperience.com, 502-475-3325

125

PRODUCTS Bulleit Bourbon, Bulleit Bourbon 10 Year Old, Bulleit Rye

Walk in the footsteps of giants: this bourbon experience is located in the former Stitzel-Weller Distillery, which opened on Derby Day in 1935 and was run by Julian "Pappy" Van Winkle for much of its history. Tours include tastes of Bulleit's high-rye whiskeys.

EVAN WILLIAMS BOURBON EXPERIENCE

528 W. Main St., Louisville, KY 40202

evanwilliamsbourbonexperience.com, 502-584-2114

PRODUCTS Evan Williams, Elijah Craig, Henry McKenna, Larceny, Bernheim Original Wheat Whiskey, Parker's Heritage Collection, William Heavenhill

If you're not thirsty before you arrive at the Evan Williams Bourbon Experience, you will be as soon as you see the giant whiskey glass fountain in the lobby. You'll see a working artisanal still that produces one barrel of bourbon per day, then sample Heaven Hill products in one of two bars: one modeled in the 1890s style, the other straight out of *Mad Men*. A Speakeasy room in the basement, entered through a faux safe door, can be rented for special events.

FOUR ROSES DISTILLERY
1224 Bonds Mill Road, Lawrenceburg, KY 40302
fourrosesbourbon.com, 502-839-3436
PRODUCTS Four Roses Yellow, Single Barrel, and Small Batch

One of the last places in the world you would expect to find a Spanish mission–style building is just off the Bluegrass Parkway near Lawrenceburg. But just like the Alamo, the bright-yellow structure and the smooth-tasting bourbon that's made here will leave an impression long after you leave. A recently expanded visitor center includes a collection of vintage advertising, antique bottles, and a premium tasting bar.

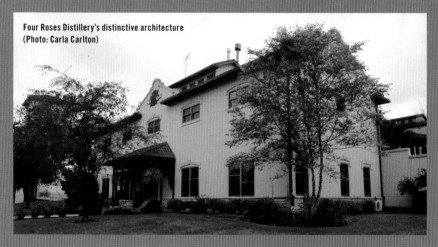

Four Roses Distillery's distinctive architecture
(Photo: Carla Carlton)

FOUR ROSES WAREHOUSE & BOTTLING
624 Lotus Road, Cox's Creek, KY 40013
fourrosesbourbon.com, 502-543-2264
PRODUCTS Four Roses Yellow, Single Barrel, and Small Batch

Alone among Kentucky distilleries, Four Roses ages its bourbon in single-story warehouses, which the company believes leads to fewer temperature variations and a smoother bourbon. You'll learn more about Four Roses' warehousing and bottling here, and then move to the tasting room to sample what's inside those bottles.

HEAVEN HILL BOURBON HERITAGE CENTER

1311 Gilkey Run Road, Bardstown, KY 40004

bourbonheritagecenter.com, 502-337-1000

PRODUCTS Evan Williams, Elijah Craig, Henry McKenna, Larceny, Bernheim Original Wheat Whiskey, Parker's Heritage Collection, William Heavenhill

The bourbons of Heaven Hill—the largest independent family-owned and -operated distilled spirits company in America—are distilled at the company's Bernheim plant in Louisville and warehoused here in Bardstown. Interactive exhibits in the Heritage Center walk you through bourbon production; after a heavenly tour of Rickhouse Y, you'll sip three samples in the Parker Beam Tasting Barrel.

Still at the Jim Beam American Stillhouse
(Photo courtesy of Beam Suntory)

JIM BEAM AMERICAN STILLHOUSE

127

526 Happy Hollow Road, Clermont, KY 40010

jimbeam.com/visit-the-bourbon-distillery, 502-543-9877

PRODUCTS Jim Beam, Baker's, Booker's, Basil Hayden's, Knob Creek, Knob Creek Rye, Knob Creek Smoked Maple, Old Grand-Dad, Jim Beam Rye, Red Stag

At the Stillhouse, which opened in 2012, you'll tour from beginning to end the production of one of the top-selling bourbons in the world. Take time to explore the grounds and snap a photo with the bronze sculpture of legendary Master Distiller Booker Noe and his faithful dog, Dot.

MAKER'S MARK

3350 Burks Spring Road, Loretto, KY 40037. (*Note:* If you're using GPS, you might have to type an extra *e* in the street name—*Burkes* Spring Road.) makersmark.com/#distillery, 270-865-2099

PRODUCTS Maker's Mark (and Cask Strength), Maker's 46 (and Cask Strength), Maker's White

Nestled on Marion County farmland, Maker's Mark is a little village built on bourbon. Restored farmhouses with crisp white gingerbread and dark brown rickhouses with neatly painted red shutters are just part of the charming experience. A recent expansion offers visitors tours, tastings, and the chance to dip your own bottle in signature red wax to take home.

TOWN BRANCH (Alltech Lexington Brewing and Distilling Co.)

401 Cross St., Lexington, KY 40508
kentuckyale.com, 859-255-2337
PRODUCTS Town Branch Bourbon, Pearse Lyons Reserve, Town Branch Rye, Bluegrass Sundown

128

This is the only stop on the trail where you can sample both craft beer—including the award-winning Kentucky Bourbon Barrel Ale—and bourbon. At 80 proof, Town Branch Bourbon is a little on the light side for my tastes; if the cask strength is available, go for that. Town Branch Rye is also nice.

WILD TURKEY

1417 Versailles Road, Lawrenceburg, KY 40342
wildturkey.com, 502-839-2182

PRODUCTS Wild Turkey 101, Wild Turkey 101 Rye, Wild Turkey 81, Wild Turkey Rare Breed, Kentucky Spirit, Russell's Reserve, Russell's Reserve Rye, Wild Turkey American Honey

The Russells—father Jimmy and son Eddie—are the highlight of a visit to this distillery perched on a Kentucky River hillside in picturesque Anderson County. If they're not on the property, you'll meet them in a heartwarming video that tells their lifelong love affair with making top-notch bourbon. A recently opened visitor center—a black structure of wood and glass—evokes the tobacco barns that once stored Kentucky's other great vice.

Visitor centers at Wild Turkey
(top) and Woodford Reserve
(Photos courtesy of Wild
Turkey and Brown-Forman)

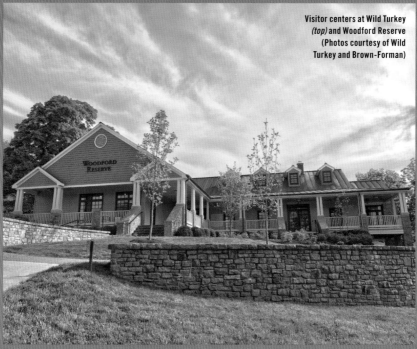

WOODFORD RESERVE

7855 McCracken Pike, Versailles, KY 40383. (*Note:* GPS will lead you to Indiana using this address, so check the map at the website below for driving directions.) woodfordreserve.com/distillery/tours, 859-879-1812

PRODUCTS Woodford Reserve Distiller's Select, Woodford Reserve Double Oaked, Woodford Reserve Rye

Past rolling hills and horse farms, you'll find one of Kentucky's oldest and most picturesque bourbon distilleries. Limestone rickhouses dot the hillside, century-old cypress fermenters bubble with mash, and the classic copper pot stills produce some of the smoothest bourbon you'll find. Take time for the culinary tasting event, where your tongue will tell you just how much chocolate, orange, and sorghum bring out different flavors of the spirit.

Other Distillery Tours

BARTON 1792 DISTILLERY

300 Barton Road, Bardstown, KY 40004

130   1792bourbon.com, 866-239-4690

PRODUCTS 1792 Small Batch Bourbon Whiskey, Limited Edition expressions

Inside Warehouse Z, where 1792 is aged, you'll see a plumb line hanging from the ceiling. The significance? Warehouse Z is a wooden warehouse, and all those 500-pound barrels of bourbon must be perfectly balanced to keep it from collapsing. If the plumb line isn't hanging straight, the warehouse manager knows things are getting out of whack—and you just might want to cut that tour short.

BUFFALO TRACE

113 Great Buffalo Trace, Frankfort, KY. (*Note*: Using GPS will get you lost, so check the website below for driving directions.) buffalotracedistillery.com, 800-654-8471

PRODUCTS Buffalo Trace, Blanton's, Eagle Rare, W.L. Weller, Elmer T. Lee, Stagg Jr., E.H. Taylor, Jr. Collection, Antique Collection, Van Winkle, Sazerac Rye

At Buffalo Trace, the wafting smell of aging bourbon—the angels' share— fills the Franklin County air as you walk the parklike grounds surrounding

Buffalo Trace warehouse
(Photo: Chad Carlton)

a working bourbon factory. The bustle of bourbon production is often on display as workers fill barrels and bottles of an impressive variety of tasty products. For an extra thrill, take the Ghost Tour, which was featured on the TV show *Ghost Hunters*—you might encounter more than alcoholic spirits.

The Kentucky Bourbon Trail Craft Tour

The following 13 distilleries made up the official Kentucky Bourbon Trail Craft Tour as of early 2017. Get a stamp from each in your passport, and you'll receive a commemorative julep cup. Each stop on the tour should have passports available, but you can also download a printable PDF at kybourbontrail.com/craft-tour. In addition, the website also has links to each distillery, where you can view their hours of operations and tour times. Because many of these distilleries have small staffs and limited space, it's always a good idea to call ahead and make sure that a particular distillery will be ready for your visit.

131

BARREL HOUSE DISTILLING CO.
1200 Manchester St., Building 9, Lexington, KY 40504
barrelhousedistillery.com, 859-259-0159

PRODUCTS Pure Blue Vodka, Oak Rum, Devil John Moonshine, RockCastle Kentucky Straight Bourbon Whiskey

Located in what was once the barreling house of the historic James E. Pepper Distillery, the appropriately named Barrel House Distilling Co. is part of a growing arts and entertainment corridor called the Distillery District. The distillery is within dribbling distance of Rupp Arena, home of the University of Kentucky Wildcats, and at the gateway of one of central Kentucky's most picturesque roads, Old Frankfort Pike.

◯ The Kentucky Bourbon Trail

1 **BULLEIT FRONTIER WHISKEY EXPERIENCE**—*Louisville*
2 **EVAN WILLIAMS BOURBON EXPERIENCE**—*Downtown Louisville*
3 **FOUR ROSES DISTILLERY/WAREHOUSE & BOTTLING**—*Lawrenceburg/Cox's Creek*
4 **HEAVEN HILL BOURBON HERITAGE CENTER**—*Bardstown*
5 **JIM BEAM AMERICAN STILLHOUSE/ URBAN STILLHOUSE**—*Clermont/Louisville*
6 **MAKER'S MARK DISTILLERY**—*Loretto*
7 **TOWN BRANCH DISTILLERY**—*Lexington*
8 **WILD TURKEY DISTILLERY**—*Lawrencburg*
9 **WOODFORD RESERVE DISTILLERY**—*Versailles*

◆ The Kentucky Bourbon Trail Craft Tour

1 **BARREL HOUSE DISTILLING CO.**—*Lexington*
2 **BLUEGRASS DISTILLERS**—*Lexington*
3 **BOONE COUNTY DISTILLING CO.**—*Petersburg*
4 **CORSAIR ARTISAN DISTILLERY**—*Bowling Green*
5 **HARTFIELD & CO.**—*Paris*
6 **KENTUCKY ARTISAN DISTILLERY**—*Crestwood*
7 **KENTUCKY PEERLESS DISTILLING COMPANY**—*Louisville*
8 **LIMESTONE BRANCH DISTILLERY**—*Lebanon*
9 **MB ROLAND DISTILLERY**—*Pembroke*
10 **NEW RIFF DISTILLERY**—*Newport*
11 **THE OLD POGUE DISTILLERY**—*Maysville*
12 **WILDERNESS TRAIL DISTILLERY**—*Danville*
13 **WILLETT DISTILLERY**—*Bardstown*

BOWLING GREEN ◇ 4

24

65

PEMBROKE ◇ 9

NEWPORT 10

NEWPORT 3

71

MAYSVILLE 11

75

CRESTWOOD 6

2 5

7

1

LOUISVILLE

64

FRANKFORT

5 PARIS

LAWRENCEBURG 9

64

8

LEXINGTON

7

CLERMONT

1 2

3

VERSAILLES

65

BARDSTOWN

4 13

LORETTO 6

DANVILLE

8

12

LEBANON

Bluegrass Distillers' horse racing–inspired logo (Photo: Carla Carlton)

BLUEGRASS DISTILLERS

501 W. Sixth St., Lexington, KY 40507
bluegrassdistillers.com, 859-253-4490

134 **PRODUCTS** Bluegrass Distillers Bourbon, Wheated Bourbon, Rye Whiskey

The yeasty aroma of mash is more than appropriate at Bluegrass Distillers' home in The Bread Box, a mixed-use redevelopment of a bakery that made Rainbo bread for more than 100 years. Friends Sam Rock, Matt Montgomery, and Nathan Brown, who opened their Lexington distillery in 2015, emphasize their location in horse country with a logo that includes jockey silks, and they've taken advantage of the nearby University of Kentucky by forming a partnership with the School of Engineering and offering internships to chemical-engineering students.

At Bluegrass Distillers, the copper pot still is also used to cook the mash. "We use one vessel for everything," Sam Rock says. "We mash two days a week, then let those ferment. We're trying to get six going at one time." They're aging for about a year in 25-gallon barrels with a high char—a method many craft distillers use to speed product, the theory being that in a smaller cask (standard barrels hold 53 gallons), the liquid will be exposed to the wood sooner. After you sample their wares, trot around to the front of the Bread Box to sample the craft beers at West Sixth Brewing, which usually has at least 15 of its own brews on tap.

Sam Rock of Bluegrass Distillers
(Photo: Carla Carlton)

135

BOONE COUNTY DISTILLING CO.

10601 Toebben Drive, Boone County (Petersburg), KY 41051
boonedistilling.com, 859-282-6545

PRODUCTS Eighteen 33 Straight Bourbon Whiskey, White Hall Bourbon Cream, Tanner's Curse White Whiskey

A cop playing the bagpipes walks into a bar. . . . no, that's not the setup for a whiskey witticism; it's how Josh Quinn and Jack Wells, partners in the Boone County Distilling Co., met each other. Josh was the piper, part of a group of police and fire personnel playing at the grand opening of an Irish pub owned by entrepreneur Jack Wells. Both men enjoyed whiskey and became interested in the stories behind the labels. In 2012, they discovered that in the 1880s, one of the largest distilleries in the nation had been located in Boone County, the county in which they lived. A Virginian named William Snyder started the Petersburg Distillery in 1833, and at the height of its production, it had an annual capacity of 4 million gallons. "Jack and I fell in love with this lost piece of local and Kentucky bourbon history," Josh says. Their Boone County Distilling Co., which opened in 2015 on 2.5 acres in an industrial park about a mile off I-75, seeks to reclaim it, starting with the name of its Kentucky Straight Bourbon: Eighteen 33.

Boone County Distilling's Eighteen 33 Straight Kentucky Bourbon (Photo courtesy of Boone County Distilling Co.)

CORSAIR DISTILLERY

400 E. Main St., #110, Bowling Green, KY 42101
www.corsairdistillery.com, 270-904-2021

1200 Clinton St., #110, Nashville, TN 37203; 615-200-0320

601 Merritt Ave., Nashville, TN 37203; 615-200-0320

PRODUCTS Artisan Gin, Red Absinthe, Vanilla Bean Vodka, Spiced Rum, Triple Smoke Whiskey, Quinoa Whiskey, Ryemaggedon; numerous seasonal and experimental spirits, including Buck Yeah, Oatrage, Grainiac, Hopmonster, and Cherrywood Smoke

Bold flavors are the trademark for this swaggering brand, which uses quinoa, buckwheat, oats, and other unusual grains in addition to corn, wheat, and barley to produce experimental spirits. Cofounder Darek Bell's philosophy at Corsair is simple: "If it's been done before, we don't want to do it." The Bowling Green distillery, the first of three Corsair locations in the Kentucky–Tennessee region, is a beautiful restoration of an old department store on the downtown square of this friendly college town.

137

Bourbon returns to Bourbon County.
(Photo: Carla Carlton)

HARTFIELD & CO.

108 E. Fourth St., Paris, KY 40361
hartfieldandcompany.com,
859-559-3494

PRODUCTS Hartfield & Co. White Whiskey, Whiskey, Bourbon Whiskey, Rum, Aged Rum, and Apple Pie Rum; experimental releases

Hartfield & Co. is literally putting the bourbon back in Bourbon County. When Andrew Buchanan and his wife, Larissa, opened their distillery in a storefront in the heart of downtown Paris in 2014, they ended a 95-year drought of distilling in the county that some people believe is the namesake of bourbon whiskey. Hartfield & Co. is using 5-gallon barrels, a tenth the size of traditional vessels, to speed-age its whiskey and bourbon.

KENTUCKY ARTISAN DISTILLERY

6230 Old LaGrange Road, Crestwood, KY 40014
kentuckyartisandistillery.com, 502-241-3070

PRODUCTS Whiskey Row Bourbon, Jefferson's Bourbon (Castle Brands),
Highspire Pure Rye Whiskey (Hope Family Wines)

In 2010, former Brown-Forman exec Stephen Thompson began bottling a blend of three whiskeys that he sourced from microdistilleries around the country; in 2014, he started distilling juice for his own brand, Whiskey Row. His business model changed when Castle Brands, which owns the Jefferson's Bourbon label, and Hope Family Wines, which owns a rye called Highspire that's aged in used wine casks, asked Kentucky Artisan to distill whiskey for them on a contract basis. Now, just over half of what the distillery produces is for Jefferson's (Highspire accounts for about 35%). Founded in 1997 by Trey Zoeller and his father, Chet, Jefferson's has never distilled its own whiskey. Instead, the Zoellers source and blend new and aged whiskeys into such sought-after releases as Jefferson's Reserve.

138

Kentucky Artisan's warehouse
(Photo courtesy of Kentucky Artisan Distillery)

KENTUCKY PEERLESS DISTILLING COMPANY
120 N. 10th St., Louisville, KY 40202
kentuckypeerless.com, 502-566-4999

PRODUCTS Lucky Kentucky Moonshine; *currently aging:* Peerless Bourbon and Peerless Rye

Just inside the flood wall on the west side of downtown Louisville, Kentucky Peerless has transformed an old tobacco auction building into a beautiful distillery. The Taylor family gutted and restored the building, salvaging floor beams and preserving the redbrick walls. Flavored moonshine (try the Chocolate Pie) is sold in what looks like old milk bottles.

Limestone Branch's barrel-stave bar (Photo courtesy of the Kentucky Distillers' Association)

LIMESTONE BRANCH DISTILLERY
1280 Veterans Memorial Highway, Lebanon, KY 40033
limestonebranch.com,
270-699-9004

139

PRODUCTS T.J. Pottinger Sugar Shine (various flavors), MoonPie Moonshine, Minor's Revenge, Precinct No. 6, Yellowstone Whiskey

When your last name is Beam, you've got a lot to live up to in the bourbon world. Fortunately, Stephen and Paul Beam evidence the skills and salesmanship of their ancestor Jacob Beam. Their beautiful boutique distillery evokes the atmosphere of small wineries of Northern California, the result of several research trips to the Napa and Sonoma Valleys before they built Limestone Branch in 2011. A partnership with St. Louis–based Luxco has returned one of the Commonwealth's most storied brands, Yellowstone, to its old Kentucky home.

MB Roland Distillery (Photo courtesy of the Kentucky Distillers' Association)

MB ROLAND DISTILLERY
137 Barkers Mill Road, Pembroke, KY 42266
mbrdistillery.com, 270-640-7744

PRODUCTS Kentucky Bourbon Whiskey, Kentucky Dark-Fired Whiskey, Kentucky White Dog, Kentucky Black Dog, True Kentucky Shine, Kentucky Apple Pie, Kentucky Pink Lemonade, flavored Kentucky Shine (Blueberry, Blackberry, Strawberry, Dark Cherry), St. Elmo's Fire, Kentucky Mint Julep

A grain silo rising out of the barrens of western Kentucky marks the territory where MB Roland Distillery produces an impressive range of spirits. The former Amish dairy farm is the cradle of operations for this destination distillery that has used concerts, crafts fairs, and family-friendly events to draw visitors. Co-owner Paul Tomaszewski said he decided to name his distillery for his wife, Mary Beth Roland, because " 'Tomaszewski' doesn't sound like a whiskey."

NEW RIFF DISTILLERY
24 Distillery Way, Newport, KY 41073
newriffdistilling.com, 859-261-7433

PRODUCTS Kentucky Wild Gin, New Riff New Make, OKI Reserve, OKI Rye Reserve, occasional special-finished bourbons

Ken Lewis is always up for a challenge. The founder and owner of The Party Source in Newport, Kentucky, the largest beverage and alcohol store

140

Event space at New Riff Distillery (Photo courtesy of the Kentucky Distillers' Association)

in the United States, decided it wasn't enough to sell other distillers' bourbons when the boom hit. So on the edge of his massive parking lot he built New Riff Distillery, complete with a 60-foot gleaming copper column still, which is visible through glass-paneled walls. He overcame the state's restrictions on owning both a distillery and a liquor store by selling The Party Source to his employees.

141

Old Pogue barrels (Photo courtesy of the Kentucky Distillers' Association)

THE OLD POGUE DISTILLERY
716 W. Second St., Maysville, KY 41056
oldpogue.com, tours@oldpogue.com

PRODUCTS Old Pogue Master's Select Kentucky Straight Bourbon Whisky, Five Fathers Pure Rye Malt Whisky, Limestone Landing Single Malt Rye Whisky

For more than 40 years before Prohibition killed the spirits, the Pogue family made whiskey in this quaint river town. Today, some of the same recipes preserved in a leather-bound journal are being distilled again at the site of the original Old Pogue Distillery. Eight Pogue family members have shifted careers—abandoning geology and supplementing oral surgery—to join the craft-distilling movement and rekindle the long-dormant family business.

Wilderness Trail products
(Photo: Carla Carlton)

WILDERNESS TRAIL DISTILLERY

4095 Lebanon Road, Danville, KY 40422
wildernesstraildistillery.com,
859-402-8707

PRODUCTS Harvest Rum, Blüe Heron Vodka; *currently aging*: Wilderness Trail Kentucky Straight Bourbon Whiskey, Settlers Select Kentucky Straight Wheat Whiskey, Settlers Select Kentucky Straight Rye Whiskey

Named for the path that pioneer Daniel Boone blazed, Wilderness Trail Distillery has its origins in science and music more than history. Two former rock-and-roll bandmates, Pat Heist and Shane Baker, first used their skills in microbiology and engineering to build a business helping other distillers perfect their yeast strains and refine fermentation practices. In 2013, they began making vodka from corn and wheat, and soon they will have more than 5,000 barrels of their whiskey aging in central-Kentucky warehouses.

WILLETT DISTILLERY

1869 Loretto Road, Bardstown, KY 40004
kentuckybourbonwhiskey.com, 502-348-0899

PRODUCTS Willett Family Estate Bottled Bourbon, Willett Family Estate Bottled Rye (aged 2, 3, 6, 7, or 8 years), Willett Exploratory Cask Finish (XCF), Willett Pot Still Reserve, Johnny Drum (Private Stock, Black Label, and Green Label), Old Bardstown (Estate Bottled, Black Label 90, Black Label 86, and Gold Label), Small Batch Boutique Bourbon Collection (Kentucky Vintage, Noah's Mill, Pure Kentucky, and Rowan's Creek)

With an exterior clad in Kentucky limestone and cedar shingles, the historic Willett Distillery outside Bardstown is one of the most beautiful in the state. The heavy wooden front doors are embellished with pulls that fit together to form a pot still, the distinctive vessel that produces the company's signature

Willett Family Estate Bottled Single Barrel Bourbon (Photo courtesy of the Kentucky Distillers' Association)

bourbon. Willett, which began distilling whiskey in 1936 and shifted to gasohol in the energy crisis of the 1970s, is firmly back in the bourbon business with an expanding campus and a host of spirits to sample.

143

Let Them Do the Driving

If you're worried about getting lost—or getting loaded—on your bourbon tour, two Louisville-based companies are ready to help you out:

MINT JULEP TOURS (mintjuleptours.com, 502-583-1433) offers a number of standing distillery tours as well as custom excursions and exclusive behind-the-scenes experiences.

R & R LIMOUSINE (rrlimo.com, 502-458-1862) lets you choose the distillery you wish to visit or designs a tour for you based on the time you have to spend.

144

146

Elk once again flourish in eastern Kentucky, where
a 16-county restoration zone was established in 1997.
(Photo courtesy of the Kentucky Department of Travel)

147

148

149

The Cumberland Gap,
a natural break in the
Appalachian Mountains,
allowed pioneers from
the East to enter the
wilderness of Kentucky.
(Photo courtesy of
the Kentucky Department
of Travel)

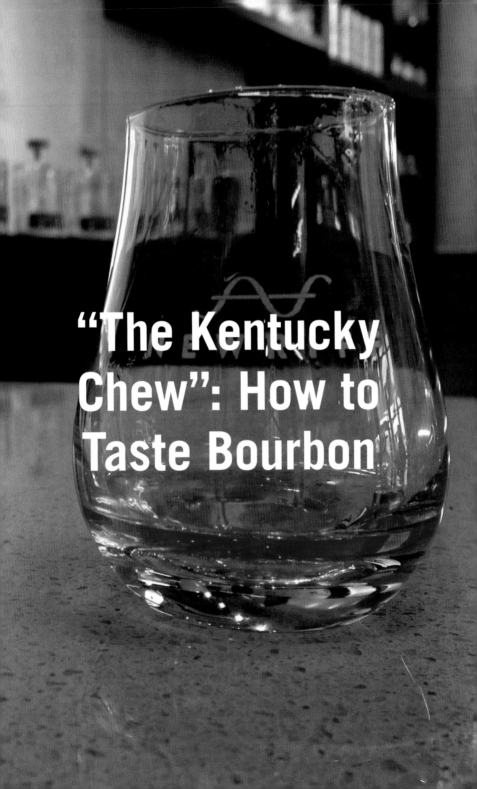

"The Kentucky Chew": How to Taste Bourbon

"A respectable amount of bourbon to pour in a glass is about two fingers' worth. Lucky for me, I have big fingers."

—*Booker T. Noe (1929–2004), Master Distiller at Jim Beam for more than 40 years*

152   IN THE FRONT YARD of the T. Jeremiah Beam House in Clermont, Kentucky, a bronze rendition of Master Distiller Booker Noe kicks back in a rocking chair, a smile on his face, a glass of bourbon in his right hand, and his faithful dog, Dot, at his left side. The white two-story frame house, built in the mid-1930s and now on the National Register of Historic Places, is smack-dab in the center of the sprawling Jim Beam Distillery, where Kentucky bourbon is produced 24 hours a day, six days a week. Until 1981, when Baker Beam moved out, the T. Jeremiah Beam House was the home of generations of Beams.

On a cool October evening, I was part of a small group that Booker's son, Fred, sporting a smile and his signature cowboy boots, welcomed for a special bourbon tasting as warmly as if he lived there still.

Frederick Booker Noe III, or Fred, as he's known, is the seventh generation of the Beam bourbon dynasty. He dealt with the obvious question first: why, then, is his last name Noe? T. Jeremiah Beam, the great-great grandson of founder Jacob Beam, had no children to whom he could pass the glass. But he did have two sisters. Margaret Beam married Frederick Booker Noe, and it was their son (and Fred's father), Frederick

Booker Noe II, who carried on the family business as the sixth-generation Master Distiller until his death in 2004. Fred Noe took on the role in 2007. His ascension to the bourbon throne wasn't preordained, though—or easy. "Booker's rule for me was, 'You finish college and we'll put you to work.' After about, oh, seven and a half years and a lot of Booker's money, I did finish college, and he did put me to work—supervising the night shift bottling line." Fred worked his way up from there.

With that short family history out of the way, he turned his attention to the tasting, encouraging us to ask questions. "If I don't know the answer, hell, I'll make one up." He began by sharing the four-step bourbon-tasting process he learned from his father:

1. **Hold the glass up and observe the color of the bourbon.** The rule of thumb is that the lighter the color, the younger the bourbon and the lighter the taste.

2. **"Nose" the bourbon.** Part your lips, rest your bottom lip on the rim of the glass, and inhale with both your nose and your mouth. That way, you don't pull in as much alcohol, and you can discern other characteristics.

3. **Taste the bourbon.** Don't toss it all back like a cowboy, though; swirl it around and let it coat all of your taste buds. According to Fred, a reporter who observed Booker working bourbon around in his mouth this way dubbed this method "the Kentucky Chew."

4. **Take note of the bourbon's finish after you swallow.** Is it smooth, or does it burn? Does the flavor linger (a "long" finish) or quickly dissipate (a "short" finish)?

We tasted the four bourbons in the Jim Beam Small Batch Bourbon Collection: Basil Hayden's, Knob Creek, Baker's, and Booker's. That order was not random; the bourbons were arranged from lowest proof (Basil Hayden's at 80) to highest, Booker's. That bourbon, which Fred refers to as "my dad's baby," is uncut and bottled at barrel strength—in this case, 130 proof. Taste that first and you're not going to taste much else after.

Booker's slides down much more smoothly than its high proof would suggest. But that doesn't mean that anyone who feels otherwise should be

153

From left: Basil Hayden's, Knob Creek, Baker's, and Booker's are on the menu at a tasting at the T. Jeremiah Beam House. (Photo: Carla Carlton)

ashamed of adding a little water or an ice cube to the glass, Fred said. "If you taste a bourbon and make a face, it's too strong," he said. "I'm giving you permission to drink my bourbon any damn way you want to."

That point underscores the main difference between a bourbon tasting and a wine tasting: the tremendous disparity in their alcohol content. Most wines have an alcohol by volume (ABV) percentage somewhere between 12% and 15%. (Rieslings tend to have a lower ABV, and fortified wines like port or sherry have higher ones.) By law, the ABV percentage of bourbon must be no less than 40, or 80 proof.

{ *Just* A SIP }

Proof is ABV multiplied by two. That means that when you tip back a glass of 80 proof bourbon, almost half of what you're drinking is alcohol—and that's the minimum. I've tasted bourbon with a proof of 140, or 70% ABV.

So proceed with caution. A woman who attended my first paid bourbon tasting learned this the hard way. She had read about the tasting in the newsletter of the store where it was being held. A veteran of wine tastings, she had never taken the first sip of bourbon, but she was eager to try something new. Before I could warn her, she picked up the glass holding our first selection, Woodford Reserve (90.4 proof), and took a big drink. She coughed. She gasped. She coughed again. Her face turned red, then

154

redder. As the other participants regarded her nervously, I started wondering if the store had a defibrillator. Fortunately, she soon recovered both her composure and her ability to breathe—and, as I recall, she bought a bottle of Woodford Reserve to take home.

{ *Just* A SIP }

I begin every bourbon tasting with a PSA: bourbon is not wine. It has much more alcohol. Unless you want to clear your sinuses, do not breathe it deeply through your nose, and when tasting, do not take a huge gulp.

Does the potency of bourbon mean it has less complexity than wine? Not at all. Brown-Forman Master Distiller Chris Morris, whose palate ensures that each bottle of Woodford Reserve has a consistent flavor profile, says his bourbon has more than 200 identifiable flavors and aromas, for example.

Bourbon has five broad areas of flavor:

- Sweet aromatics (caramel, vanilla, butterscotch, for example)
- Woods and nuts (oak, cedar, pecan, walnut)
- Grains (corn, rye, malt)
- Fruit and floral notes (berries, cherries, apple, honeysuckle, rose petals)
- Spices, both brown (nutmeg, coffee, tobacco, pepper) and savory (licorice, spearmint)

155

You won't find all of these flavor notes in every glass, of course. And it may take you a while to pick up subtler nuances. When I started making bourbon tasting notes, they often went something like this: "Vanilla . . . caramel . . . ummmm . . . oak? That's all I got."

For me, the fruity notes are often the most elusive. The first time I heard someone mention banana as a possible flavor note, it sounded like the start of a bad joke: "Waiter, there's a banana in my bourbon." I mean, really. *Banana?* Then, several years ago, I asked Jean Neighbors, a bartender for 35 years at the Jockey Silks Bourbon Bar in Louisville, to bring me something I might not have tried before. She placed a glass of Johnny Drum in front

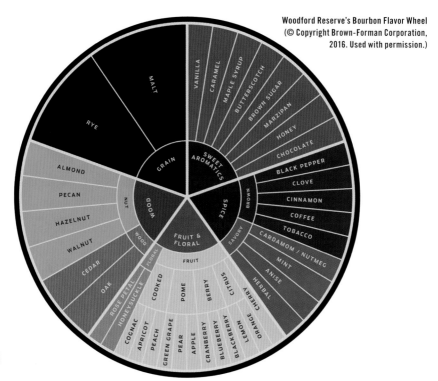

Woodford Reserve's Bourbon Flavor Wheel
(© Copyright Brown-Forman Corporation,
2016. Used with permission.)

of me. I picked it up and nosed it—and, sure enough, the predominant aroma was banana.

I can't identify all 200 flavors and aromas in Woodford Reserve, but over the years I have developed my palate far beyond the recognition of just vanilla, caramel, and oak. You can, too. And the good news is that the best way to do so is to drink more bourbon. Here are some tips.

Develop a tasting vocabulary. When you have a list of possible flavors and aromas in front of you, you can better identify exactly what you're smelling or tasting. You won't be limited to saying a bourbon tastes "nutty," for instance; you can pinpoint the kind of nut—pecan, or almond, or hazelnut, for example.

Familiarize your nose and palate with the nuances you might find in bourbon. If you don't know what allspice smells like or what cooked apricot tastes like, you won't be able to identify those notes in the flavor profile of a bourbon. Most of the flavor components aren't terribly exotic; you probably have most of the spices in your kitchen right now.

Do some advance research. Look up the brand on the company's website and see if the Master Distiller's tasting notes are listed. Make a copy. The next time you taste that bourbon, use the notes as a guide and see if you can discern those flavors and aromas.

Take a flight. A cost-effective way to sample several bourbons at one time is to order a bourbon flight, which usually consists of three or four half-ounce pours. I asked Chris Morris for advice on how to select the components of a flight. "You don't want to try a variety of bourbons, like Maker's and Woodford and Booker's. You'll be able to tell the big differences, because they are very different, but you very quickly are going to lose the subtleties because of the alcohol content," he said. "It's like saying, 'I'm going to try a Zinfandel, a Pinot Noir, and a Cabernet Sauvignon.' You're going to get confused." He recommends tasting "families" of bourbons—three Wild Turkey expressions, for instance, or three products from Four Roses—and seeing how they differ. Servers at a good bourbon bar will be able to make flight suggestions.

Choose the correct glass. At a bourbon bar, you're likely to be served in a crystal Glencairn glass. Shaped like a tulip, it gives the bourbon room to open up, and it narrows at the top, which focuses the aroma and allows you to nose it above the glass. Glencairn glasses look impressive, too. But don't feel that you have to run out and buy a bunch of them; the standard rocks glass will work as well. Really, the only glass that isn't recommended

157

Glencairn glasses await a tasting at Heaven Hill's Bourbon Heritage Center in Bardstown, Kentucky. (Photo courtesy of the Kentucky Distillers' Association)

for a tasting is a shot glass. Designed for quick delivery, shot glasses emphasize the burn, not the bouquet.

Take it for a swirl. As Fred Noe suggests, hold up your glass and examine the color of the bourbon, which can range from straw to amber to a deep reddish-brown. Generally, the darker the bourbon, the older it is, and therefore the higher the proof will be. Then, gently swirl the contents of the glass. Swirling allows some of the alcohol vapors to dissipate, so that you'll pick up more of the bourbon's aromas when you nose it. Interestingly, what you smell may not match what you taste. Some bourbons have a luscious nose that their flavor can't match, and vice versa. Now, take a sip and swirl the liquid around your mouth. See which parts of your tongue "light up." We sense sweetness front and center, bitter on the back, and savory on the edges. Does the bourbon have a thick, chewy mouthfeel, or is it thin? Pay attention to the finish. Is the flavor still there several minutes later, or does it dry up as soon as you swallow?

Hold your water. Taste a new bourbon neat (without water or ice) first, so that you experience it fully. Then, if you find it too strong, add a splash of water. Even if it's not too warm for you, you might want to add a drop or two of water. This opens up many bourbons, and it can emphasize or deemphasize certain flavor notes. Some bourbons also open up as the heat from your hand warms them.

158

{ *Just* A SIP }

While I sometimes enjoy drinking bourbon on the rocks, I don't recommend adding ice cubes when you're doing a tasting, because they can immediately deaden some of the nuances, and then dilute everything as they melt. In any case, do have a glass of water nearby, and maybe some bland crackers, so that you can cleanse your palate between samples.

After a few sessions, you might want to **try a blind tasting,** where you don't know which bourbons you're sampling, to see what you can discern. You may not be able to identify exact brands this way (there are so many!), but soon you'll be able to tell if the mash bill contains rye or wheat, and make a pretty accurate guess as to the age of the sample.

159

A tasting glass focuses the aromas of bourbon and lets you nose it above the rim.
(Photo courtesy of the Kentucky Distillers' Association)

The tasting bar at Corsair Artisan Distillery in Bowling Green, Kentucky, offers samples of more than a dozen of its spirits. (Photo: Carla Carlton)

Limit your tastings to no more than four small pours. Bourbon's high alcohol content will not only confuse your palate, it will also raise your blood-alcohol level quicker than you might imagine. Bring along a designated driver, or call a cab if you overdo it.

Finally, remember that **when it comes to bourbon, there are no wrong answers.** Everyone's palate is different. You may not taste everything that the person next to you does. And even if you do, you may not like that bourbon as much. And that's OK. As you sample more bourbons, you'll start to learn which ones you like, and as your palate evolves, you'll be able to give voice to what it is you like about them. Before you know it, you'll be using descriptors like "tannic" and "herbal" and "marzipan."

Or maybe you won't.

Longtime Wild Turkey Master Distiller Jimmy Russell always says he uses "simple terms" to describe bourbon's flavor—like the vanilla and caramel notes in his Russell's Reserve 10 Year Old. He likes to tell a story about the time that he and the late Buffalo Trace Master Distiller Elmer T. Lee, another legend of the industry, attended a tasting event. They sat there, listening, as the speaker rhapsodized about the flavors in a particular whiskey: dried fruit, chocolate, pepper, leather.

"Elmer leaned over to me," Jimmy recalls with a twinkle, "and he said, 'You ever put any of that shit in your bourbon?' "

160

MOST BOURBON IS GOOD. WHAT MAKES A BOURBON *GREAT*?

People often ask me what my favorite bourbon is. My standard reply is "Kentucky bourbon." I'm not trying to be diplomatic; it's just too difficult to narrow it to one! That being said, the bourbons that I most enjoy—the ones I place in the "excellent" category—have certain qualities in common:

They have a complex, inviting nose in which I discern multiple notes. I'm especially drawn to bourbon that combines the best of the woody characteristics (caramel, vanilla) with some dark fruit and a bit of spice.

That complexity continues when I take a sip. As the liquid touches different parts of my palate, its character evolves—it's as if the bourbon "blooms" on my tongue. In a truly great bourbon, no one flavor dominates; there is a wonderful balance of sweet and spice. I prefer a thick, "chewy" mouthfeel to a thin one.

The finish is long and warming, with no afterburn and no tannic bitterness. For this reason, I typically don't like overaged bourbon (no, not even Pappy 23). It's tough to avoid the more bitter aspects of the barrel after so much evaporation has occurred—although it can be done. Wild Turkey Tradition, a 14-year-old limited edition released in 2009, for instance, is one of the best bourbons I've ever tasted, and one of the very few that prompted me to go on the hunt for additional bottles.

One thing to keep in mind, though, is that with today's bourbon, "most expensive" doesn't always equate to "best." Even the bottles on the bottom shelf are pretty darned good.

161

A bourbon bar, such as Bourbons Bistro in Louisville, Kentucky, which serves more than 130 brands, is a good place to try a bourbon flight, or sampler. (Photo courtesy Bourbons Bistro)

Double-Barreled: Betting on Bourbon's Future

"Today's rain is tomorrow's whisky."

—*Scottish proverb*

ON THE SEVENTH FLOOR of Warehouse Y at Heaven Hill in Bards-town, it's already steamy. Even on a fairly mild day for June in Kentucky, the temperature at 8 a.m. is 80 degrees and rising, and the bourbon in the barrels up here has started its morning stretch into the wood. Through spaces between the planks underfoot, you can see the barrels on the sixth floor that are similarly occupied, and the fifth, and the fourth, all the way down to the first floor, where it's slightly cooler and the bourbon might be sleeping in.

The sweet, syrupy aroma of bourbon envelops you, tickling your nose, as it rises from all 20,000 barrels to the top floor and then beyond toward the angels. At any one time, 1.2 million barrels are biding their time at Heaven Hill, the liquid at their centers intensifying in flavor and color until the Master Distillers determine it has matured enough to exit the casks in an amber-colored cascade.

The same scenario is playing out at distilleries across Kentucky, where 6.6 million barrels are aging—the most since 1974. Distillers have ramped up production, doubling it in some cases, in response to the world's enthu-siasm for bourbon, which is almost as palpable as that angels' share.

Warehouses at Heaven Hill Distillery
(Photo courtesy of Heaven Hill)

But will the world still be as thirsty 4, 8, 10, or 12 years from now? Bourbon producers certainly hope so. Since 2000, they've more than doubled their annual production, from 572,000 new barrels to 1.89 million in 2015. In the past four years alone, they have put up more than 5 million new barrels. But their business is unlike almost any other in today's fast-food, instant-gratification culture: it takes a long time. The barrels they fill today aren't just containers—they're time capsules.

{ *Just* A SIP }

"If you want to get rich quick," says Wild Turkey Master Distiller Jimmy Russell, "find out a way that you can make a four-year-old bourbon taste like a six-year-old bourbon. Speed up the aging on it. . . . Everything you can think of has been tried, but it's Mother Nature that has to take care of it."

The nature of his business has taken on added poignancy for Wild Turkey's Jimmy Russell, who turned 82 in November 2016. Today, when he watches bourbon dumped into the barrel, he's not really thinking about how well it will eventually sell, he says. "I tease the young people: 'You know what I'm hoping now? At my age, I hope I'm still around when it's put in the bottle.' "

167

Bottling line at Woodford Reserve Distillery
(Photo courtesy of Brown-Forman)

Master Distillers of Russell's generation have seen how planning can miss the mark on both ends of the spectrum. During the last boom, in the 1950s and 1960s, producers wildly overestimated the lasting appeal of their product, resulting in a huge glut when drinkers' tastes had turned to lighter spirits like vodka by the time the bourbon was ready to bottle.

But as bourbon's reputation began to soar again, some companies made decisions that proved to be too cautious. "In 2006, I started every managers meeting by saying, 'We are not putting enough barrels away,'" says Jim Rutledge, former Master Distiller at Four Roses. "We were just getting outside Kentucky [with sales], but the interest in Four Roses was amazing." On his first trip to San Francisco, for example, he met with a small group of spirits writers and connoisseurs. "I went back a month or two later, and all these restaurants wanted me to come. It wasn't showing up in numbers yet, but I could feel the momentum. I described it this way: 'We are this little-bitty tiny snowball at the top of a mountain, just beginning to roll. If we don't start right now preparing for when we get down here, we're not going to be able to stop it.'

"I was accused of being too optimistic, too passionate. But I used to do the long-range planning for all Seagram's distilleries—I know how to do it. I said I wasn't being too optimistic. And besides, I'd rather be too optimistic than pessimistic, because you can always adjust downward. You can shut the distillery down a couple months early. But if you come up short, well, I've never learned how to make six-year-old bourbon tomorrow."

No one listened, he said. "In 2011, our case sales increased by 42% over 2010. In 2012, we jumped 58% over 2011. In 2013, we were up 71% over that. But they were still saying, 'This can't last—this is just an anomaly.' Well, then, in 2014, we ended up 78% over the 71%." As a result, Four Roses had to curtail growth to put more bourbon away to age, and bottle some bourbon that was a bit younger than usual. Rutledge retired in September 2015 and was succeeded by Brent Elliott. "It will be Brent that brings us out of it," Rutledge said shortly before he stepped down.

The promotion of Elliott, who has worked at Four Roses since 2005, is the most recent in a series of shifts in management at venerable Kentucky distilleries. In 2010, Rob Samuels succeeded his father, Bill Samuels Jr., as chief operating officer of Maker's Mark. When the late Parker Beam stepped down as Master Distiller at Heaven Hill in 2013 after the announcement that he had ALS, the company promoted Denny Potter, manager of its Bernheim Distillery, to be co–Master Distiller with Parker's son, Craig Beam. The following year, Eddie Russell joined his father, Jimmy, as co–Master Distiller of Wild Turkey. And at Jim Beam, the eighth generation of that storied bourbon-making family, Freddie Noe IV, has joined the company.

These newcomers—a term I use facetiously, since many of them have worked for their companies for decades—are steeped in the traditions and taste profiles of their respective brands. They certainly know how to make whiskey. But they are taking over at a time of unprecedented growth, and they will have to make the decisions about future production.

"I think a lot of people are seeing it now: How can you prepare for something no one's seen before?" says Brent Elliott. "That's the million-dollar question. But what bourbon has apart from other categories or products is that the growth is backed up by a solid foundation of tradition, quality, and craftsmanship, and these aren't characteristics that go out of fashion."

Still, planning is tricky when you're dealing with something as subjective as the public's tastes. Can bourbon sustain its recent remarkable trajectory? "We're banking that it's going to be sustainable—literally," says Buffalo Trace's Harlen Wheatley. Do you have your to-do list filled in for the next 23 years? Wheatley does. He knows which products the distillery will be making through the year 2039—and some of them are already in the barrel.

"We're probably better right now than we were in the '50s and '60s, when bourbons were really strong, which is super for all of us," Wild Turkey's Eddie Russell says in *Kentucky Bourbon Tales,* produced by the Nunn Center for Oral History and the KDA. "It's a great thing because of who our consumer is now. Our consumer has always been an older gentleman, and now it's 25- to 40-year-old males and females that's growing our industry."

Women are also taking more visible leadership roles in bourbon. Michter's Distillery promoted 18-year industry veteran Pam Heilmann to the position of Master Distiller in late 2016, making her one of Kentucky's first female Master Distillers since Prohibition. Another is Marianne Barnes, who studied under Brown-Forman's Chris Morris before becoming Master Distiller at the new Castle & Key Distillery, which is taking shape on the grounds of the historic Old Taylor Distillery just outside Frankfort, Kentucky. Barnes barreled her first bourbon in December 2016 and plans to release gin and vodka in 2017. Bourbon created by a woman "will appeal to a different segment of the market," she says.

Another reason the industry is so bullish on bourbon this time around is that, unlike in previous booms, interest isn't limited largely to the United States. "There is one thing going for us that we didn't have in the '70s and '80s—the international markets," says Eric Gregory, KDA president. "We can barely keep up with demand now. You add in China, India—that is why distilleries are quadrupling production."

Overseas sales could also help smaller craft distilleries survive, says John Pogue of Old Pogue Distillery, a microdistillery in Maysville, Kentucky. "Publicly traded companies must sell overseas. That will lead to shelf space for us smaller guys. I think it's pretty close to how the craft-beer industry took off. It's showing the same trend. And craft beer is only at about 10% of the total market. It's mind-boggling. There's still a long ways to go."

{ *Just* A SIP }

Nationally, the market share of spirits made by microdistillers is just around 2% by volume, but the American Distilling Institute, a trade group, says that if current trends continue, that share could be as large as 8% by 2020.

Paul Tomaszewski of MB Roland Distillery in Pembroke, Kentucky, also makes the craft-beer connection. "People ask me, 'What about when the craft-distillery movement goes bust?' Has craft beer gone bust? It's gone up and down, don't get me wrong, but there are more coming on all the time. The smaller ones are getting big, and the bigger ones are getting bought out. We are barely flirting with the tip of the iceberg in a lot of ways."

He also notes that size is relative. Some older people who have visited his distillery are frustrated when they ask when they'll be able to buy his products in their states, and his response is, "You can't."

"They've been spoiled by the big distillers who can snap their fingers and have their stuff in 50 states. I'm never going to be in 50 states. I'll be lucky if

Marianne Barnes, Master Distiller at
Castle & Key Distillery in Frankfort,
Kentucky (Photo: Matt Malicote/
Malicote Photography)

172

KENTUCKY
MINT
JULEP 33% ALC/VOL

PEMBROKE CHRISTIAN CO. KY 66 PROOF

This is the original Mint Julep. Dating back over two centuries ... weight & wood ... retaining the grand old tradition, premium Liquor ... of Kentucky ...

liqueur

TRUE
KENTUCKY
SHINE 50% ALC/VOL

PEMBROKE CHRISTIAN CO. KY 100 PROOF

MBR

This is an entirely authentic recipe of white corn & cane sugar copper pot distilled in small batches honoring the centuries-old traditions of those that came before us in the Commonwealth of Kentucky

spirits distilled from 50% corn & 50% cane sugar

MB Roland, which began in 2009 with a 100-gallon pot still, has upsized to a 600-gallon still. (Photo courtesy of the Kentucky Distillers' Association)

I'll be in 10. We've actually had people give us poor reviews online because we were out of bourbon when they visited. It's a unique situation. But I'm quite pleased and really excited about the younger folks who are getting into it. The millennials and the Gen Xers think this is cool and fun and neat and interesting. They're willing to roll with it. It's like single-malt Scotch. You've got several obscure bottlings and brands that you can't get everywhere, and you're never going to get them everywhere. We're going to be a white elephant: if you see it and you want it, you probably should buy it."

Younger consumers are also the ones who are most attracted to small artisanal operations like microdistilleries, Pogue says. "You see it in food places, too. Like in Oregon [where Pogue worked as a geologist before coming to Kentucky to be a distiller], little markets are just thriving. Those personal relationships—I don't think that will go away. I have that sentiment, too. I enjoy my local coffee shop and my local butcher."

Of course, not all of the small distilleries that are cropping up across the country will make it. In a 2015 update on the craft-distilling industry for ADI, research economist Michael Kinstlick noted that while the overall number of small distilleries has increased from 234 to more than 1,000 since his first such white paper was published in 2012, there have also been enough "exits" that he is beginning to amass data on those as well. These exits occur either for a happy reason—the craft distillery is bought by a larger company—or, more likely, a sad one—the distiller can no longer afford to continue an enterprise that can take years to break even, much less to make a profit.

173

"You start off and you're so wide-eyed," says Tomaszewski, who opened his distillery in 2009. "You get your first stuff bottled and shipped out, and everyone is so excited. And I'm thinking, 'Just wait.' After someone has been doing it about a year or so, their attitude and the way they talk is very different. The reality sets in: this is gonna take a while. I call it 'the 1,000-gallon stare.' "

But even if the bourbon wave crests, Kentucky has a growing attraction that no other state can claim: bourbon tourism that rests on a foundation of 200 years of history and heritage. More than 1 million people are expected to visit at least one distillery experience in Kentucky in 2017, "and I think we are still very early in the tourism game—a 2 or 3 on a scale of 10," says

Louisville mayor Greg Fischer. "We know about it locally, but the world is just getting to know about it. And when people come, their expectations are exceeded. It's not just about having a drink of bourbon; it's much broader. It's the history, the art, the people behind it, the pastoral settings and the urban settings. It's something that is uniquely ours."

Jim Rutledge is expressing his confidence in bourbon in a very concrete way: in May 2016, he announced that he plans to open his own distillery near Louisville.

"I think we are just scratching the surface. People around the world have begun to realize there's another whiskey in this world besides Scotch, and it's Kentucky bourbon. We have years and years and years of growth to even come close to catching up. You look back at about 1968, when our barrel inventory in Kentucky was close to 9 million. Probably 90%–95% of that was for domestic consumption. We're at about 6 million now—but 40% of that 6 million will be used in international markets. That leaves just 3.6 million for domestic consumption. Look at the difference just to catch up.

"I'm very optimistic for the industry. That, to me, is the most important message that needs to go out from here: our industry is here to stay."

Kentucky's seasonal changes aren't just beautiful—they also play a role in bourbon maturation. (Photo courtesy of the Kentucky Department of Travel)

A pour of Old Pogue Master's Select Kentucky Straight Bourbon
(Photo courtesy of the Kentucky Distillers' Association)

APPENDIX A
From Alligator Char to White Dog: A Glossary of Bourbon Terms

"Stop your nonsense and drink your whiskey!"

—Zachary Taylor, when a Whig first suggested that Taylor run for president. Taylor, president from 1849 to 1850, grew up near what is now Louisville and is buried in the Zachary Taylor National Cemetery there.

ALLIGATOR CHAR The deepest level at which the inside of a barrel is charred—No. 4 on a scale from 1 to 4—so called because the blistered surface resembles the cracked skin of an alligator.

ANGELS' SHARE The amount of bourbon that evaporates during the aging process, typically 2%–4% per year.

BACKSET The thin liquid that remains after a batch of whiskey mash is distilled. A portion is added to the next batch when making sour mash whiskey to ensure consistent flavor (sort of like sourdough bread starter). Also known as *setback, stillage, spent beer,* or, if the distiller prefers the sweet-mash method, *slop.*

BARREL PROOF/BARREL STRENGTH Describes bourbon bottled straight from the barrel, with no water added. Also known as *cask strength.*

BEER STILL See *column still.*

BOTTLED-IN-BOND Under the Bottled-in-Bond Act of 1897, bourbon that is produced in one distillation season by one distiller at one distillery; aged for at least four years in a government-bonded warehouse; and bottled at

100 proof with nothing added but water. The act was designed to protect consumers from unsavory folks who were bottling all sorts of stuff at the time and calling it whiskey. Today, that really isn't an issue, and brands that draw attention to the fact that they meet the bottled-in-bond requirements do so mostly as a marketing practice.

BRANCH WATER Water taken from a stream, or branch; the mixture of bourbon and water is sometimes referred to as *bourbon and branch.*

BRAND NAME Term that originated in the 1830s when it became common for distillers to burn, or "brand," their names on their barrelheads.

BUNG The stopper in a barrel. Bungs are typically made of poplar, which swells when wet for a tight seal, although Maker's Mark uses walnut.

BUNG KNOCKER The hammer used to hit a chisel to remove the bung; it resembles a small sledgehammer. The term also makes a good epithet ("You bung knocker!").

CHARRING The process by which the interior of a barrel is set fire to for less than a minute to caramelize the wood and create a layer of char that will act as a filter for the whiskey. Distillers can choose from four levels of char.

CHILL-FILTERED Describes whiskey that has been chilled and passed through a series of filters to remove esters, fatty acids, and proteins before bottling so that it doesn't cloud when water or ice is added to a glass. This is an issue only with whiskeys that are 46% ABV (alcohol by volume) or lower; a higher alcohol content prevents the cloudiness from occurring. Producers who favor chill-filtering say consumers view a cloudy whiskey as inferior. Those opposed say that removing the natural by-products of distilling dilutes the flavor.

COLUMN STILL A tall metal column, usually copper or stainless steel, fitted inside with a series of perforated horizontal plates that separate alcohol from water during first distillation. Also called a *continuous still or beer still.*

CORN WHISKEY Whiskey made from a mash bill containing a minimum of 80% corn. Corn whiskey is often not aged, but if it is, used or uncharred oak barrels must be used. Also known as *corn liquor* or *white lightning.*

DEVIL'S CUT The several gallons of bourbon that are lost because they have soaked into the walls of the oak barrel. See *Sweating the barrel,* page 182.

178

DIRTY WATER A common slang term for bourbon. Also known as *brown water*.

DISTILLER'S BEER The thick, fermented liquid that enters the beer still for first distillation.

DOUBLER A copper still used for the second distillation of whiskey that removes impurities and concentrates the alcohol.

FINGER A rough measurement of bourbon—the width of a finger, or about 1 ounce.

FINISH What you continue to smell, taste, and feel after you swallow bourbon.

FINISHING Changing or enhancing the flavor of bourbon by additional aging in a second barrel—sometimes in another oak barrel, as with Woodford Reserve Double Oaked, but often in a barrel that has been used to age a fortified spirit such as port wine (Angel's Envy) or sherry (Jim Beam Distiller's Masterpiece sherry cask–finished bourbon). Because these spirits are no longer technically bourbon because a flavor has been added, distillers must specify this on the label.

HEADS The first 5% of so of the alcohol to evaporate during distillation. High in undesirable compounds such as methane, the heads are condensed, collected, and discarded.

HEARTS The second, and longest, percentage of the alcohol collected during distillation, this is the whiskey that will be barreled and aged.

HIGH WINES Term for the liquid that emerges from a doubler following second distillation.

HONEY BARREL Slang term for a particularly tasty barrel of bourbon or whiskey that will likely be bottled as a single barrel. Also called *sugar barrel*.

LEGS The streaks that cascade down the inside of your bourbon (or wine) glass after you swirl it, the legs result from the fact that alcohol in bourbon evaporates faster than the water in it. When you swirl, the alcohol tries to escape, only to be pulled back in by the water. A lot of legs can indicate a high alcohol content.

LOW WINES The liquid that goes into a doubler after first distillation.

MASH Mixture of cooked grains and water to which yeast is added to begin fermentation.

MASH BILL The grain recipe for bourbon or other whiskey.

MASH TUB The large container where milled grains are cooked in water in order to break their starches down into the sugar that yeast will feed on during fermentation. Also known as a *cooker*.

MOONSHINE A fanciful name that some distillers put on their labels to evoke the early days of distilling; there is no official TTB definition (see page 182) for moonshine. If the spirit is made from sugar, it's classified as rum; if it's made from a grain, it can be a whiskey if it follows the guidelines. If it is made from both sugar and grain, the TTB must approve the formula and will define the class based on the mash bill. Ironically, most moonshines on the shelf today are legally rum.

NEAT Bourbon served with no ice or water.

NOSE The aroma of a bourbon.

POT STILL Another type of whiskey still. Heat is applied directly to the pot containing the mash, and the resulting alcohol vapors travel through a condensing coil. Because the spent mash must be cleaned out each time, this is known as *batch distilling* rather than continuous distillation.

PROOF The measure of alcohol in a spirit. In the United States, it's expressed as double the percentage of the alcohol by volume (ABV). An 80 proof bourbon, therefore, is 40% ABV.

RICKHOUSE The building in which the barrels of whiskey are aged. Also called a *warehouse* or *rackhouse*.

RICKS The wooden shelflike structures on which barrels of whiskey rest during aging.

ROCKS Same as on the rocks: over ice.

RYE WHISKEY Whiskey made from a mash bill that is at least 51% rye, distilled at a maximum of 160 proof, and aged at no more than 125 proof in new charred-oak barrels.

SETBACK See *backset*.

SINGLE-BARREL WHISKEY Whiskey bottled from one barrel that has not been mingled with any other whiskeys.

181

SMALL-BATCH WHISKEY Whiskey that has been produced by mingling the juice from several barrels. There is no official definition for small-batch; it might contain whiskey from 4 barrels or 40 barrels, for example. It's up to the distiller.

SOUR MASH/SWEET MASH Two methods for making whiskey or bourbon. In the sour-mash method, which is used by all major bourbon producers in Kentucky, a portion of the backset, or thin liquid that remains after distillation, is added to the next batch of mash during fermentation to balance pH levels and ensure consistency from batch to batch. In the sweet-mash method, a brand-new batch is produced each time, with nothing set back.

STRAIGHT BOURBON/STRAIGHT WHISKEY Whiskey that has been aged for a minimum of two years.

STRAIGHT UP/UP Sometimes considered interchangeable, these terms actually have different meanings. *Straight up* is another term for ordering bourbon neat, with no ice. *Up* refers to a drink that is shaken with ice, then strained into a glass with a stem, like a martini glass.

SWEATING THE BARREL A process to reclaim some of the devil's cut (see page 177).

TAILS The last segment of alcohol to come off the still, this low-proof liquid still contains usable alcohol but also has some impurities. It's captured and later redistilled.

THUMPER Another type of still used for the second distillation of American whiskey (see *doubler*), this gets its name from the thumping sound made when the alcohol vapors bubble through water. This sound doesn't occur in a doubler because the alcohol being refined is already in liquid form.

TOASTING A lighter level of heat applied to the inside of a barrel or barrelhead that helps to mellow the tannins and release vanillins and other flavors. Sometimes done in an oven rather than over an open flame.

TTB Alcohol and Tobacco Tax and Trade Bureau, the federal agency that protects the public by enforcing provisions of the Federal Alcohol Administration Act and collects taxes on distilled spirits.

WASH See *distiller's beer*.

WHEAT WHISKEY Whiskey made from a mash bill that is at least 51% wheat, distilled at a maximum of 160 proof, and aged at no more than 125 proof in new charred-oak barrels. Not to be confused with wheated bourbon (see below).

WHEATED BOURBON Bourbon with a mash bill that contains wheat as the secondary grain, rather than rye, making it softer and sweeter. Also referred to as a *wheater*.

WHISKEY THIEF A long "straw," often made of copper, used to draw whiskey from a barrel for sampling.

WHITE DOG Bourbon in its clear state as it leaves the still. Also known as *unaged whiskey* or *new make*.

Thieving some whiskey at Corsair Distillery in Bowling Green, Kentucky (Photo courtesy of the Kentucky Distillers' Association)

183

APPENDIX B
Classic Cocktails:
Recipes and Stories of
the Old-Fashioned, the Manhattan,
the Seelbach Cocktail, and the Mint Julep

"Pluck the mint gently from its bed, just as the dew of the evening is about to form on it. Select the choicer sprigs only, but do not rinse them. Prepare the simple syrup and measure out a half-tumbler of whiskey. Pour the whiskey into a well-frosted silver cup, throw the other ingredients away, and drink the whiskey."

—*Mint julep recipe attributed to Henry Watterson (1840–1921), Pulitzer Prize–winning editor of* The Courier-Journal, *Louisville, Kentucky*

Bourbon punch at The Eagle Food & Beer Hall in Louisville
(Photo courtesy of the Louisville Convention and Visitors Bureau)

The Old-Fashioned

In this drink's original incarnation, it was called simply a whiskey cocktail and consisted of a little sugar, a few dashes of bitters, whiskey, and a twist of lemon over ice. That's how purists still make it. The drink became known as the old-fashioned around the turn of the 20th century, and that's when it started to get tarted up with fruit on the rim of the glass. At some point after Prohibition, bartenders began muddling the fruit into the drink.

It was pretty much off the bar menu when *Mad Men* premiered in 2007, but Don Draper, whose very first line of dialogue was an order for another old-fashioned, helped to revive it. I like a bit of fruit in my old-fashioned, but I'm not a big fan of muddling. And I don't add club soda or any water beyond what's needed to dissolve the sugar a bit—the old-fashioned is all about the bourbon.

OLD-FASHIONED

½ tsp. sugar (or a sugar cube)

2–3 dashes bitters (I like to use Regan's Orange Bitters No. 6, which gives a nice hint of orange without being too sweet)

A couple of drops water

½ orange

2–2 ½ oz. good bourbon (Old Forester for an OF², or Old Forester old-fashioned)

Orange or lemon slice for garnish

Put the sugar in an old-fashioned glass. Moisten with the bitters and water. Squeeze in a bit of orange, peel it, and throw in the peel. Add the bourbon. Stir. Add a couple of cubes of ice and stir again. Garnish with an orange or lemon slice. If you really want a cherry in there, I recommend Woodford Reserve Bourbon Cherries or Luxardo cherries.

187

The Manhattan

This cocktail dates to the 1880s. Unlike the old-fashioned, it never went totally out of style, but like all classic cocktails, it's much more in demand now than it has been for several decades. Considerably less sweet than the old-fashioned, it's traditionally mixed with rye whiskey, but these days it's just as acceptable to request that it be made with bourbon.

Here's a fun fact: at one time, there were cocktails named for all the New York City boroughs. The other one made with whiskey is called the Brooklyn—where the Manhattan includes sweet vermouth and bitters, the Brooklyn calls for whiskey, dry vermouth, and cherry liqueur. The Bronx and the Queens are gin-based, and the Staten Island Ferry is equal parts rum and pineapple juice. All but the Manhattan became obscure after Prohibition.

MANHATTAN

¾ oz. sweet vermouth
2½ oz. bourbon
1–2 dashes Angostura bitters
1 cherry

Combine everything but the cherry with a few ice cubes in a mixing glass. Stir—**do not shake!**—for about 8 seconds. Place the cherry in the bottom of a well-chilled cocktail glass, and strain the bourbon mixture over the cherry.

189

The Seelbach Cocktail

For 20 years, the story behind this bubbly bourbon-and-Champagne concoction was that a bartender at the historic Seelbach Hotel in Louisville, Kentucky, had discovered and revived a pre-Prohibition recipe for what had once been the hotel's signature drink. It was a great story, repeated by more than a few cocktail writers. But in October 2016, Adam Seger, the bartender, admitted that he'd made the whole thing up—the story and the drink. "I felt the hotel needed a signature cocktail," he told *The New York Times*. "How could you have a place that F. Scott Fitzgerald hung out in that doesn't have a damn cocktail?" Well, now it does—and you shouldn't let fiction get in the way of the fizz.

SEELBACH COCKTAIL
1 oz. bourbon (The Seelbach uses Old Forester)
½ oz. Cointreau
7 dashes Angostura bitters
7 dashes Peychaud's bitters
5 oz. Champagne
Orange twist

Chill a Champagne flute. Add the bourbon first, followed by the Cointreau and two kinds of bitters. Top with Champagne and garnish with an orange twist.

191

The Mint Julep

Everyone should be fortunate enough to attend the Kentucky Derby at least one time. If fortune does thus smile upon you, do not—I repeat, *do not*—let anyone at Churchill Downs peer-pressure you into buying a mint julep. The julep's PR team has done a terrific job of convincing the general population that this drink is de rigueur at the Derby, but the ones served at the track are sickeningly sweet and too minty—sort of like drinking mouthwash.

To me, those mint juleps—and honestly, most of the ones I've sampled anywhere over the years—fail the first requirement of a good bourbon cocktail: *you must be able to taste the bourbon.* If you really want to try a julep, I recommend having a reputable bartender at a good place build one just for you. You can also make a julep at home if you have access to fresh 'Kentucky Colonel' spearmint.

Here's a recipe from Chris Zaborowski, co-owner of Westport Whiskey & Wine in Louisville.

MOM'S MINT JULEP

½ cup fresh mint leaves
1 part Mom's Simple Syrup (recipe follows; prepare several days before needed)
2 parts good bourbon (Chris's mom always used Old Forester)
1 mint sprig

"Spank" the mint in the palm of your hand and drop it into a cup, preferably a silver julep cup. (Be careful with the mint: if you're too rough—in other words, if you muddle it—you'll release bitter flavors along with the mint's sweetness.) Fill the cup with finely crushed ice (think snow-cone texture), and pour in the simple syrup and bourbon. Stir gently for 10–15 seconds until a frost forms on the outside of the cup. Garnish with a mint sprig.

Mom's Simple Syrup

1 cup cold water
2 cups sugar
½ cup fresh mint leaves
1 oz. good bourbon (optional)

Combine the water and sugar in a saucepan. Cook 5 minutes at a soft boil, using a candy thermometer as a temperature guide. Add the mint leaves, remove from heat, add the bourbon (if desired), and let steep at least 12 hours. Strain into a pitcher. Makes enough for 5–6 juleps.

193

WHIS

DISTILLERS · REC

MAIN STRE

The Evan Williams Bourbon Experience celebrates the history of Louisville's Whiskey Row. (Photo courtesy of Heaven Hill)

One of eight original warehouses on the Willett Distillery property just outside Bardstown, Kentucky (Photo courtesy of the Kentucky Distillers' Association)

INDEX

206

Barrels rest at the Jim Beam American Stillhouse in Clermont, Kentucky. (Photo courtesy of Beam Suntory)

207

ABOUT THE AUTHOR

CARLA HARRIS CARLTON is an award-winning bourbon journalist and speaker who covers the industry on her website, **TheBourbonBabe .com**, which draws readers from around the globe and has been featured on NPR's *All Things Considered* and in *The Washington Post* and *The New York Times*. She is also a founding member of Bourbon Women, a networking organization for women who are passionate about exploring bourbon and its culture.

A native of Louisville, Kentucky, Carla worked at the *Courier-Journal* for nearly two decades before joining the Office of Communications & Public Affairs at Bellarmine University, a private liberal-arts university that claims Bill Samuels Jr. of Maker's Mark as a trustee. Carla comes by her taste for whiskey honestly: her grandmother worked the bottling line at Seagram's in Louisville in the late 1930s, and her grandfather grew his own mint for his yearly Derby Day julep. Her collection of Kentucky bourbon memorabilia is surpassed only by her collection of Kentucky bourbon. She lives in Louisville with her husband, Chad; their children, Harper and Clay; and their dog, Tyler.

Still thirsty?

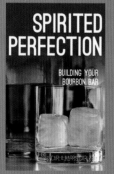